Lecture Notes in Business Information Processing 477

LNBIP reports state-of-the-art results in areas related to business information systems and industrial application software development – timely, at a high level, and in both printed and electronic form.

The type of material published includes

- Proceedings (published in time for the respective event)
- Postproceedings (consisting of thoroughly revised and/or extended final papers)
- Other edited monographs (such as, for example, project reports or invited volumes)
- Tutorials (coherently integrated collections of lectures given at advanced courses, seminars, schools, etc.)
- Award-winning or exceptional theses

LNBIP is abstracted/indexed in DBLP, EI and Scopus. LNBIP volumes are also submitted for the inclusion in ISI Proceedings.

Cristina Cabanillas · Francisca Pérez

Editors

Intelligent Information Systems

CAiSE Forum 2023
Zaragoza, Spain, June 12–16, 2023
Proceedings

 Springer

Editors
Cristina Cabanillas ⓘD
Universidad de Sevilla
Seville, Spain

Francisca Pérez ⓘD
San Jorge University
Zaragoza, Spain

ISSN 1865-1348   ISSN 1865-1356 (electronic)
Lecture Notes in Business Information Processing
ISBN 978-3-031-34673-6   ISBN 978-3-031-34674-3 (eBook)
https://doi.org/10.1007/978-3-031-34674-3

This Springer imprint is published by the registered company Springer Nature Switzerland AG
The registered company address is: Gewerbestrasse 11, 6330 Cham, Switzerland

Preface

The CAiSE conference series provides a platform for exchanging experiences, preliminary research results, and ideas between academia and industry in the field of information systems engineering. The conference serves as the annual worldwide meeting point for the community of information system engineers. The 35th edition of the CAiSE conference was organized by the SVIT research group at San Jorge University, and held in Zaragoza, Spain, during June 12–16, 2023. This edition of the conference put a special emphasis on the theme of Cyber-Human Systems.

The CAiSE Forum is a place at the CAiSE conference for presenting and discussing new ideas and tools related to information systems engineering. Intended to serve as an interactive platform, the Forum aims to present emerging topics and controversial positions, and demonstrate innovative systems, tools, and applications. The Forum sessions facilitate the interaction, discussion, and exchange of ideas among presenters and participants. Similar to other recent Forum editions, two types of submissions were invited in 2023:

- *Visionary papers* present innovative research projects, which are still at a relatively early stage and do not necessarily include a full-scale validation.
- *Demo papers* describe innovative tools and prototypes that implement the results of research efforts.

Each submission to the Forum was reviewed by at least two Program Committee (PC) members. The submissions that achieved a consensus on relevance, novelty and rigour were accepted for presentation at the Forum. Of the 25 submissions received, 12 were invited to the Forum from the CAiSE main research track and had already undergone the peer review process of the conference. Nonetheless, each such invited paper was reviewed by two PC members, too. All those papers were accepted. Six of the 13 new submissions (46%) were accepted after the peer review process of the Forum. Altogether, 18 papers were accepted at the CAiSE 2023 Forum, and were presented at dedicated sessions of the CAiSE conference. The accepted papers are collected in this volume.

We want to thank all the contributors to the CAiSE 2023 Forum. Firstly, we thank the PC members for their timely and high-quality reviews and help promoting the event. Secondly, we thank the Program Chairs of the CAiSE conference, Iris Reinhartz-Berger and Marta Indulska, for their assistance with handling the papers invited from the main research track. Thirdly, we thank all the authors of the papers for sharing their work with the community. Fourthly, we thank Pierluigi Plebani for his support with the preparation of the Forum proceedings. Finally, we thank Carlos Cetina and Oscar Pastor, the General Chairs of the CAiSE 2023 conference, and the conference's Local Organizing Committee for their support in coordinating the paper presentations at the conference and their publication.

June 2023   Cristina Cabanillas
                                                              Francisca Pérez

Organization

Chairs

Cristina Cabanillas   University of Seville, Spain
Francisca Pérez   San Jorge University, Spain

Program Committee Members

Abel Armas Cervantes	The University of Melbourne, Australia
Corentin Burnay	University of Namur, Belgium
Cinzia Cappiello	Politecnico di Milano, Italy
Maya Daneva	University of Twente, The Netherlands
Johannes De Smedt	KU Leuven, Belgium
Jānis Grabis	Riga Technical University, Latvia
Marite Kirikova	Riga Technical University, Latvia
Henrik Leopold	Kühne Logistics University, Germany
Andrea Marrella	Sapienza University of Rome, Italy
Pierluigi Plebani	Politecnico di Milano, Italy
Manuel Resinas	University of Seville, Spain
Anthony Simonofski	Université de Namur, Belgium
Tijs Slaats	University of Copenhagen, Denmark
Arnon Sturm	Ben-Gurion University, Israel

Contents

Context-Aware Change Pattern Detection in Event Attributes of Recurring Activities

Jonas Cremerius$^{(\boxtimes)}$ and Mathias Weske

Hasso Plattner Institute, University of Potsdam, Potsdam, Germany
{jonas.cremerius,mathias.weske}@hpi.de

Abstract. Process mining bridges the gap between process management and data science by utilizing process execution data to discover and analyse business processes. This data is represented in event logs, where each event contains attributes describing the process instance, the time the event has occurred, and much more. In addition to these generic event attributes, events contain domain-specific event attributes, such as a measurement of blood pressure in a healthcare environment. Taking a close look at those attributes, it turns out that the respective values change during a typical process quite frequently, hence we refer to them as *dynamic event attributes*. This paper studies change patterns of dynamic event attributes by recurring process activities in a given context. We have applied the technique on two real-world datasets, MIMIC-IV and Sepsis, representing hospital treatment processes, and show that the approach can provide novel insights. The approach is implemented in Python, based on the PM4Py framework.

Keywords: Process Mining · Change Pattern Detection · Recurring Activities · Context-Aware

1 Introduction

Business organisations take advantage of data-driven approaches to better understand and improve their processes. By logging process execution data, a tremendous amount of data is available. Process mining allows analysing this data by extracting event logs from information systems, which can be used for process discovery, conformance checking, and enhancement [1]. Traditionally, process mining methods and techniques focus mainly on the activities executed during a process, and their execution dependencies, such as ordering. More recently, data has entered centre stage in process mining, extending traditional process discovery and enhancement techniques.

Investigating event logs in detail, we find that certain activities create attribute values, for instance, laboratory values representing a patient's state during a hospital stay. These activities might be executed several times in a given treatment process, such that the respective attribute changes multiple

C. Cabanillas and F. Perez (Eds.): CAiSE 2023, LNBIP 477, pp. 1–8, 2023.
https://doi.org/10.1007/978-3-031-34674-3_1

times. We call these attributes dynamic event attributes [7]. This characteristic of dynamic event attributes is particularly interesting, as it allows analysing their change patterns [6]. Process models can then be enhanced by the change patterns, allowing to get additional process-oriented insights.

In typical healthcare treatment processes, certain activities (e.g., measurements) occur several times. We could study changes of event attributes, but we cannot relate those changes to the process context. In this paper, we present an approach that allows us not only to detect change patterns of activities, but to also relate those changes to the process context. Thereby, we can study the effect of treatment activities on the resulting measurement values, which, at least in healthcare processes, is instrumental.

The remainder of this paper is organized as follows. Section 2 provides related work, and Sect. 3 motivates the problem. Section 4 presents the approach dealing with recurring activities, and Sect. 5 applies the approach to two different datasets. The paper is concluded in Sect. 6.

2   Related Work

In this section, we present research dealing with the analysis of dynamic event attributes and event log preprocessing.

In [6], the authors propose a method to detect change patterns in dynamic event attributes by applying statistical tests on event attribute values of activity pairs, which are in a directly or eventually follows relation and have one or more event attributes in common. Change pattern detection is highly present in time series data, which refers to the problem of finding abrupt changes in data when a property of the time series changes [2]. However, time series change detection accepts only one value per time point, which leads to information loss and lacks a detailed representation of the analysed group [2].

Whereas the identification of change patterns between activities is rather new, event log preprocessing is an established research area, offering a broad range of techniques [12].

Event log preprocessing techniques can be grouped into two major types, transformation, and detection techniques. Whereas transformation techniques modify the event log, detection techniques perform grouping, such as trace clustering [12]. This paper focusses on transformation techniques, which are mostly based on filtering. Lots of research focusses on infrequent behaviour or detection of anomalies [4,5]. Additionally, there exists research dealing with activities happening at arbitrary points in time, which are defined as chaotic activities [15].

There is also research dealing with refining event labels to discover more precise process models. In [10], the authors derive duplicated events from the control-flow perspective and enumerate the events. Time and further event attributes can also be considered to include the semantic of events for refining event labels [14].

In this paper, we look into the problem of identifying change patterns in event attributes of recurring activities. On the one hand, this is a problem for the change pattern detection, as the only relevant directly/eventually follows relation is the activity to itself. On the other hand, event log preprocessing techniques either filter events or refine event labels by enumeration or time, but do not relate them to other activities, i.e., to the context.

3   Foundations and Motivating Example

Before presenting the approach, we introduce preliminaries on events and event logs, and we motivate our work using an example.

Let V be the the universe of all possible values and A be the universe of event attributes. An event e is a mapping of event attributes to values, such as $e \in A \rightarrow V$. The universe of events is defined by $E = A \rightarrow V$. If an event $e \in E$ has no value assigned to an event attribute $a \in A$, it is denoted as $e(a) = \perp$. A trace $t \in E^*$ is a sequence of events. $T \subseteq E^*$ represents the respective universe of traces, in which all events are unique. An event log L is a set of traces, so $L \subseteq T$.

Normally, an event represents an activity conducted within a certain case at a given time, the latter of which is represented by a timestamp. These properties of events are represented by the event attributes activity (act), caseID, and timestamp. The events of a given trace have the same value for the caseID attribute, and they are ordered by their respective timestamps. For simplicity, we assume that two timestamps of events in a given trace are never equal.

Given events $e_i \neq e_j$ in a given trace t, let $e_i > e_j$ represent a directly follows relationship, if e_j appears after e_i and there does not exist an event e_k in t which appears between e_i and e_j, where $e_k \neq e_i \wedge e_k \neq e_j$.

The goal of this paper is to identify context-aware change patterns for recurring activities with event attributes. We define change patterns as statistically significant increases or decreases of event attribute values between activities in a process for the respective cases in the event log conducting these activities [6].

Table 1. Example event log describing activities conducted in an intensive care unit (ICU).

Case ID	Activity	Timestamp	Creatinine
1	**Perform blood test**	1	8
1	**Perform blood test**	2	9
1	Start dialysis	3	/
1	**Perform blood test**	4	4
1	End dialysis	5	/
1	**Perform blood test**	6	1.5

It can be observed from the example event log illustrated in Table 1 that the activity "Perform blood test" is the only activity that includes additional event attributes, namely a lab value. As the activity is performed multiple times, the event attribute **creatinine** is said to be *dynamic* and changes throughout the process execution [7]. As the event attribute is only attached to one activity

("Perform blood test"), methods for change pattern detection in dynamic event attributes consider all changes from the activity to itself [6]. For example, the following changes of **creatinine** are considered: $8 \rightarrow 9, 9 \rightarrow 4, 4 \rightarrow 1.5$

This is a problem, because it is difficult to derive a common behaviour of event attributes, as the context of the recurring activity is not considered. For example, dialysis is known to lower the **creatinine** value, which is not detected by this method, as it considers all value changes, no matter where these were observed [13]. Thus, we cannot evaluate, if activities result in an improvement or worsening of conducted measurements, neglecting the chance of finding important insights about the treatment process. Next, we provide an approach to overcome this problem by relating event attribute changes to the context.

4   Approach

In the following, we provide a technique to detect recurring activities semi-automatically. Second, we transform recurring activities to provide context-aware change pattern results. The approach will be explained along the motivating example illustrated in Table 1.

4.1   Recurring Activity Detection

Before recurring activities can be transformed to be suitable for change pattern detection, we need to detect these first. We define recurring activities as activities, that occur between the usual control flow multiple times. This is illustrated in Table 1, where "Perform blood test" is present through the whole process. We propose to express that by measuring, if an activity is mainly preceding and following other activities, and thus, occurring in multiple contexts within the process. To calculate this, we introduce a modified directly-follows and directly-precedes ratio, as proposed by [15].

Given two activities $a, b \in \alpha$, with $\alpha \subseteq V$ denoting the set of activities in L, we define $dfr(a, b, L)$ as the ratio of how often an event with activity a is followed by an event with activity b relative to the occurrence of b in a given event log L. $\#(a, L)$ provides the number of occurrences of activity a in L and $\#(a > b, L)$ denotes the number of occurrences of the directly follows relation $a > b$.

$$dfr(a, b, L) = \frac{\#(a > b, L)}{\#(b, L)} \tag{1}$$

Please note, that a and b in the directly follows relation $a > b$ are events with the respective activity name, such that $a(act) = a$ and $b(act) = b$.

$dpr(a, b, L)$ is defined as the ratio of how often an event with activity a is preceded by an event with activity b relative to the occurrence of b in L:

$$dpr(a, b, L) = \frac{\#(b > a, L)}{\#(b, L)} \tag{2}$$

As proposed in [15], we calculate both ratios for all activities in the event log.

Given an activity $a \in \alpha$, $dfr(a, L)$ and $dpr(a, L)$ are vectors including the results of each $dfr(a, b, L)$ and $dpr(a, b, L)$ respectively for all $b \in \alpha$.

By dividing the occurrence of the given traces by $\#(b, L)$ instead of $\#(a, L)$, we know if a is primarily following or preceding **other** activities. When a is recurring, it acts like a central point in the process, which is often followed or preceded before the usual control flow is continued.

We propose to take the mean value of the vector values in $dpr(a, L)$ and $dfr(a, L)$ for all activities $a \in \alpha$, resulting in a repetition score rep_a:

$$rep_a = \frac{\sum dpr(a, L) + \sum dfr(a, L)}{|\alpha| * 2} \tag{3}$$

The activities with the highest scores and at least one *dynamic* event attribute available should be considered as potential candidates for recurring activities. The classification of recurring activities is a semi-automatic step, where significant higher values in rep_a should be considered as potential candidates. We argue, that setting an arbitrary threshold to detect those completely automatically might result in wrong classifications, as an activity $a \in \alpha$ could be recurring only at a part of the process, such that $dfr(a, L)$ has high values for 50% of the activities and is 0 for the rest. This results in two sets of activities, where $\alpha^r \subseteq \alpha$ includes recurring activities and $\alpha^{nr} \subseteq \alpha$ includes non-recurring activities, where $\alpha^r \cup \alpha^{nr} = \alpha$ and $\alpha^r \cap \alpha^{nr} = \emptyset$.

4.2   Context Identification and Event Transformation

To identify the context of interest, we propose to consider the frequency of the activity execution in the given context. Therefore, we assume that it is of interest to analyse a recurring activity $a \in \alpha^r$ at activities, which are often following or preceding the recurring activity. We define two sets $\rightarrow_a, \leftarrow_a$, where $\rightarrow_a$ includes the activities $b \in \alpha^{nr}$ preceding a sufficiently often and $\leftarrow_a$ includes the activities, where b is following a sufficiently often:

$$\rightarrow_a = \{b \in \alpha^{nr} \mid dpr(a, b, L) \geq \lambda\} \tag{4}$$

$$\leftarrow_a = \{b \in \alpha^{nr} \mid dfr(a, b, L) \geq \lambda\} \tag{5}$$

We argue, that choosing the threshold depends on the process under investigation, which should be seen again as a form of guidance to identify activities in the process being affected by recurring activities.

Next, we will transform the events in L according to the activities in $\rightarrow_a$ and $\leftarrow_a$ to allow a context-aware analysis of recurring activities.

We propose to rename the activity names of events representing recurring activities according to their context. The context can be before or after a non-recurring activity, which is represented by $\rightarrow_a$ and $\leftarrow_a$ for a recurring activity a. Thus, we take all events representing a being directly before or after a non-recurring activity, where the context should be analysed. This is formalized as follows. Let $t \in L$ be a trace:

$$\epsilon_{\rightarrow_a} = \{e \in t \mid \exists e_1 \in t \colon e_1 > e \land e_1(act) \in \rightarrow_a \land e(act) = a\} \tag{6}$$

$$\epsilon_{\leftarrow_a} = \{e \in t \mid \exists e_1 \in t \colon e > e_1 \land e_1(act) \in \leftarrow_a \land e(act) = a\} \tag{7}$$

After that, the event log is filtered to only include events representing context-specific recurring activities and all other non-recurring activities:

$$t' = \{e \in t \mid e \in \epsilon_{\rightarrow_a} \lor e \in \epsilon_{\leftarrow_a} \lor e(act) \in \alpha^{nr}\} \tag{8}$$

To relate recurring activities to the context, we concatenate their activity names with activities happening **before** or **after** them. Thus, the activity names of events in $\epsilon_{\rightarrow_a}$ are renamed to a **after** the directly preceding event $e \in t'$ with $e > a$. Respectively, the activity names of events in $\epsilon_{\leftarrow_a}$ are renamed to a **before** the directly following event $e \in t'$ with $a > e$, which is illustrated in Table 2, where the concatenation is displayed by the $\cdot$ notation.

Table 2. Transformed event log describing activities conducted in an ICU

Case ID	Activity	Timestamp	Creatinine
1	Perform blood test · **before** · Start dialysis	2	9
1	Start dialysis	3	/
1	End dialysis	5	/
1	Perform blood test · **after** · End dialysis	6	1.5

The new event log L' includes then all modified traces t'. Table 2 shows a possible transformation of the log illustrated in Table 1, where $\rightarrow_a$ includes all "Start" activities and $\leftarrow_a$ all "End" activities, assuming that in most traces "Perform blood test" occurred before and after treatment activities. We can now analyse the relation ("Perform blood test before Start dialysis", "Perform blood test after End dialysis") instead of taking all blood tests into account. With that, the **creatinine** decrease due to dialysis can be detected. One can now also see, if blood tests are performed before or after an activity for each case when discovering a process model.

5   Evaluation

In this section, we evaluate if the proposed approach can detect recurring activities and provide context-aware insights regarding changes in event attribute values. To do that, we compare the results of the original change pattern detection, as proposed in [6], to the context-aware approach on two real-world healthcare datasets (MIMIC-IV and Sepsis) [9,11]. The datasets were chosen based on their availability of recurring activities with event attributes. The approach is implemented in Python with the help of the PM4Py framework and is publicly available on GitHub[1] [3]. Due to limited space, we can only present the results for Sepsis. A detailed description of the datasets and visualization of the results and process models is available in the GitHub repository.

[1] https://github.com/bptlab/Context-Aware-Change-Pattern-Detection.

First, we want to confirm the assumption that recurring activities are often followed or preceded by other activities in the process. For Sepsis, prominent candidates are "CRP" ($rep = 0.17$) and "Leucocytes" ($rep = 0.16$), which are exactly the recurring measurements in the event log. Surprisingly, "Lactic Acid" ($rep = 0.06$), which is also a measurement activity, has a similar score as other non-recurring activities. After further investigation, we identified, that "Lactic Acid" is mostly performed once per case. Thus, we also did not consider this as a recurring activity. The results of Sepsis are especially interesting, as the recurring activities do not occur throughout the whole process, but only partially, which explains the lower score. In the end, the expected recurring activities had a considerably higher repetition score and could be detected. For Sepsis, most values of dfr/dpr were around 0.05, where only a few were above the manually chosen threshold of $\lambda = 0.18$, which shows, that there exist contexts, where the measurements are conducted more frequently. We also observe that the differentiation between dfr and dpr is important, as the measurements are sometimes only conducted before or after a non-recurring activity, such as the activity "Release A", where the measurements are only conducted before that.

Table 3. Summary of change patterns for Sepsis

Relation	P	Effect Size (**RBC**)	Mean values
CRP AFTER ER Sepsis Triage, CRP AFTER Admission NC	0.0009	0.29	121.63 → 130.66
CRP AFTER Admission NC, CRP BEFORE Release A	2.39×10^{-47}	−0.97	147.6 → 60.49
CRP AFTER Admission IC, CRP AFTER Admission NC	0.041	−0.43	183.13 → 118.37
CRP AFTER ER Sepsis Triage, CRP BEFORE Release A	2.49×10^{-7}	−0.54	119.42 → 66.43
Leucocytes AFTER ER Sepsis Triage, Leucocytes AFTER Admission NC	7.65×10^{-9}	−0.52	13.88 → 11.32
Leucocytes AFTER Admission NC, Leucocytes BEFORE Release A	7.95×10^{-11}	−0.45	13.85 → 12.65
Leucocytes AFTER ER Sepsis Triage, Leucocytes BEFORE Release A	4.02×10^{-7}	−0.55	12.97 → 10.48

Table 3 shows identified change patterns, which are independent of a certain trace variant. It can be observed, that, dependent on where the measurements are conducted, the change patterns differ. For example, looking at the CRP measurements, CRP has a tendency to increase from "CRP AFTER ER Sepsis Triage" to "CRP AFTER Admission NC" and then drastically decreases from "CRP AFTER Admission NC" to "CRP BEFORE Release A" for almost all patients with an effect size of −0.97. That shows, how important the context is, as the effect of the treatment takes some time to decrease the CRP value [16]. Leucocytes has a decreasing pattern throughout the whole process, which is also expected to decrease [8]. The number of statistically significant changes ($p < 0.05$) increased from one to 14 in comparison to the original event log, revealing different change patterns dependent on the context. We observe a similar improvement for the MIMIC event log. This presentation shows, that recurring activities can be detected and that a context-aware perspective provides novel insights regarding their value and process behaviour.

6 Conclusion and Future Work

This contribution researches methods to deal with recurring activities including additional information in the form of event attributes by transforming them into context-aware activities. This allows to detect change patterns of the event attribute values dependent on the context in which the recurring activity is conducted. We have shown, that according to the context, change patterns can be different, providing novel insights for event attributes of recurring activities.

Future work could research methods for detecting recurring activities and their context fully automatically. Furthermore, other metrics could be suitable for the detection, such as the eventually follows ratio, and other ways of determining recurring activities could be researched, e.g., by looking at the distribution of repetition scores.

References

1. van der Aalst, W.: Process Mining. Springer, Heidelberg (2016). https://doi.org/10.1007/978-3-662-49851-4
2. Aminikhanghahi, S., Cook, D.J.: A survey of methods for time series change point detection. Knowl. Inf. Syst. **51**(2), 339–367 (2017)
3. Berti, A., et al.: Process mining for python (PM4Py): bridging the gap between process-and data science. CoRR abs/1905.06169 (2019)
4. Bezerra, F., Wainer, J.: Anomaly detection algorithms in logs of process aware systems. In: Proceedings of the 2008 ACM Symposium on Applied Computing, SAC 2008, pp. 951–952. Association for Computing Machinery, New York (2008)
5. Conforti, R., Rosa, M.L., Hofstede, A.H.T.: Filtering out infrequent behavior from business process event logs. IEEE Trans. Knowl. Data Eng. **29**(2), 300–314 (2017)
6. Cremerius, J., Weske, M.: Change detection in dynamic event attributes. In: Di Ciccio, C., Dijkman, R., del Río Ortega, A., Rinderle-Ma, S. (eds.) BPM 2022, pp. 157–172. Springer, Cham (2022). https://doi.org/10.1007/978-3-031-16171-1_10
7. Cremerius, J., Weske, M.: Supporting domain data selection in data-enhanced process models. In: Wirtschaftsinformatik 2022 Proceedings 3 (2022)
8. Farkas, J.D.: The complete blood count to diagnose septic shock. J. Thorac. Dis. **12**(Suppl. 1), S16–S21 (2020)
9. Johnson, A., et al.: MIMIC-IV. In: PhysioNet (2022)
10. Lu, X., Fahland, D., van den Biggelaar, F.J.H.M., van der Aalst, W.M.P.: Handling duplicated tasks in process discovery by refining event labels. In: La Rosa, M., Loos, P., Pastor, O. (eds.) BPM 2016. LNCS, vol. 9850, pp. 90–107. Springer, Cham (2016). https://doi.org/10.1007/978-3-319-45348-4_6
11. Mannhardt, F.: Sepsis Cases - Event Log (2016). https://data.4tu.nl/articles/dataset/Sepsis_Cases_-_Event_Log/12707639
12. Marin-Castro, H.M., Tello-Leal, E.: Event log preprocessing for process mining: a review. Appl. Sci. **11**(22), 10556 (2021)
13. Schiffl, H.: Discontinuation of renal replacement therapy in critically ill patients with severe acute kidney injury: predictive factors of renal function recovery. Int. Urol. Nephrol. **50**(10), 1845–1851 (2018)
14. Tax, N., Alasgarov, E., et al.: Generating time-based label refinements to discover more precise process models. J. Ambient Intell. Smart Environ. **11**(2), 165–182 (2019)
15. Tax, N., Sidorova, N., van der Aalst, W.: Discovering more precise process models from event logs by filtering out chaotic activities. J. Intell. Inf. Syst. **52**(1), 107–139 (2018)
16. Yentis, S.M., Soni, N., Sheldon, J.: C-reactive protein as an indicator of resolution of sepsis in the intensive care unit. Intensive Care Med. **21**(7), 602–605 (1995)

Towards a UML Profile for Designing Smart IoT Data-Centric Applications

Houssam Bazza[1], Sandro Bimonte[2](✉) ⓘ, Julian Eduardo Plazas[3] ⓘ,
Laure Moiroux Arvis[2], Hassan Badir[1], Juan Carlos Corrales[3] ⓘ,
and Stefano Rizzi[4] ⓘ

[1] IDS, Abdelmalek Essaadi University, Tangier, Morocco
houssam.bazza@etu.uae.ac.ma, hassan.badir@uae.ac.ma
[2] TSCF, INRAE Clermont-Ferrand, 9 avenue Blaise Pascal, Aubière, France
{sandro.bimonte,laure.arvis}@inrae.com
[3] GIT, Universidad del Cauca,, Popayán Cauca, Colombia
{julian.plazas,carlos.corrales}@unicauca.ma
[4] University of Bologna, Bologna, Italy
stefano.rizzi@unibo.it

Abstract. The implementation of IoT (Internet of Things) systems is difficult since the data sent from the devices is complex, especially in agriculture and agroecology, where it is generated from heterogeneous hardware and software, and its applications involve different actors. In this scenario, conceptual design is mandatory to provide a formal and unambiguous representation allowing the different actors to set their requirements. The problem with the current representations is that they do not take into account neither the internal parameters nor the dynamic aspect of smart devices. To fill this gap we propose SmartSTS4IoT, an extension of the STS4IoT UML profile that models the different representations of internal/external data expressed from the same sensor and the logic used to adapt the sending/sensing policies to sudden environmental changes. The profile is illustrated with reference to a case study in the context of smart agriculture and validated theoretically.

Keywords: Internet of Things · UML profile · smart sensors

1 Introduction

Internet of Things (IoT) is a widely used technology. It is based on the convergence of wireless technologies, acquisition devices (sensors, smartphones, vehicles, etc.), and the internet to provide decision-makers with real-time data issued from different locations. Recent advances in the electronic and hardware components of IoT devices have led to a new, smarter kind of devices that goes beyond a basic data-sending functionality by incorporating some computation capabilities (ranging from simple rules to AI). So these smart devices can dynamically change their data sensing and sending behavior according to internal and/or external data. This leads to pushing intelligence down, in a real-time and distributed

© The Author(s), under exclusive license to Springer Nature Switzerland AG 2023
C. Cabanillas and F. Perez (Eds.): CAiSE 2023, LNBIP 477, pp. 9–16, 2023.
https://doi.org/10.1007/978-3-031-34674-3_2

way, at the devices level [17], thus opening perspectives for the development of many applications in several areas, such as health, traffic, smart building, and agriculture. Although IoT systems offer new important possibilities, their implementation is still difficult and time-consuming since (i) the data sent from smart devices are complex (real-time spatio-temporal stream data), and (ii) their implementation requires the interaction of various actors (decision-makers, sensors, data and network experts), who must be able to understand each other to clearly specify their functional and non-functional requirements, as well as the technological means [10].

Some recent works investigate the usage of software engineering methodologies for IoT [10]. In particular, conceptual design has been recognized as a mandatory activity for a successful implementation of complex systems. Several formalisms have been proposed to this end. Recently, the use of UML for the conceptual design and automatic implementation of IoT-based data-centric applications has been proposed [14]. The authors present a UML profile that allows to describe the IoT data used by any application by means of simple UML Class diagrams. The main idea is to provide IoT experts and decision-makers with an unambiguous formalism (UML) they can use to discuss and converge toward an implementation that satisfies the functional and non-functional requirements of the application. However, the profile proposed does not explicitly model the inner logic governing the behavior of smart devices.

To fill this gap, in this work we extend the profile proposed in [14] to allow different representations (including sensing and sending policies) of the data issued from the same IoT device. This allows defining explicitly the logic used to change the representation by means of OCL or other UML diagrams. Our proposal, named *SmartSTS4IoT*, represents a framework allowing the actors of IoT applications to discuss and converge towards shared and feasible requirements before the implementation step. Our claim is that representing smart devices at a conceptual level can guide and help IoT experts in the choice of the right technologies and their correct deployment.

The paper is structured as follows: Sect. 2 motivates our proposal by means of a case study in smart agriculture; Sect. 3 discusses the related work; Sect. 4 presents the SmartSTS4IoT profile; finally, Sect. 5 gives a theoretical evaluation of SmartSTS4IoT and draws the conclusions.

2   Requirements for Designing Smart IoT Applications

In this section, we list the requirements that our conceptual model should support, using smart agriculture as a representative scenario [5].

With the advent of IoT, agriculture is moving towards a digital transformation and new tools are being developed to optimize the management of farms and harvests with a low level of human intervention. IoT is not limited to the deployment of simple measurement sensors for precision agriculture, but it comes with on-board intelligence that provides valuable assistance to decision-makers. For example, to optimize water consumption, sensors coupled with an intelligent irrigation system are used to automatically plan the irrigation of a plot. Thus, the intelligence provided by IoT allows better knowledge and control of agricultural operations. In this paper we consider as running example the monitoring of fires in fields.

Internal Parameters. The air temperature sensors are deployed in open fields, far from agricultural buildings, and they are powered by batteries. It is important to alert the farmers when the battery level is too low, in order to plan a human intervention in the field to promptly replace the batteries. Thus, first of all, a conceptual model for smart IoT should support the representation of *internal parameters* of the devices that must be communicated over the network (the battery level in this case).

State-Dependent Behavior. A sensor can operate in different states, and it will move from one state to another following the application of rules; depending on the state of the sensor, it can manage different data. As an example, consider the IoT application in charge of alerting farmers when a fire is burning. A temperature exceeding a given threshold (say 27 Celsius degrees) could mean that a fire is starting. However, before a fire prevention action is launched, a more accurate monitoring should be started to prevent false alarms. Thus, the temperature could be measured by end nodes every minute rather than every 30 min for some time and for all sensors in the field. Besides, the data sent from these end nodes should be compared inside a sink node to verify that they are coherent, i.e., that high temperature values are not erroneous. The logic used by nodes to change sensing and sending policies is crucial in these applications, so its formal representation is necessary to let the different actors involved agree on a solution. Sensor states can even be associated to different data acquisition policies. For example, in presence of high temperatures, air humidity should be monitored as well; thus, a device can manage different data at different times.

Data-Centric Representation. As stated in [14], the dynamic aspects of devices should be represented in the same diagram used for data, because they have a great impact on the semantics of the data collected and sent. This representation should also be well understandable, since the actors involved in the design and implementation of these systems have different skills (for example, farmers and experts in sensors, databases, and networks).

3   Related Work

IoT technologies are mature enough to provide effective solutions to real life problems. However, their conceptual design has not been sufficiently studied by the academic and industrial communities. A conceptual representation for IoT has been investigated in several works, mostly focused on the design of physical component of the IoT system, i.e., on the *internal parameters* requirement. From the point of view of *state-dependent behavior*, few works have been proposed. Some works focus on the conceptual design of intelligence rules inside devices. For instance, in [9] a Model-Driven Architecture (MDA) approach is proposed to improve the interoperability among IoT devices so as to ensure better data compatibility. In [15] the authors propose to combine mashup and model-based development, and represent the behavior of IoT components using UML Activity and State diagrams. A design architecture for representing the dynamic components for cyber-physical systems is introduced in [13], by distinguishing different types of smart devices. The possible components of a smart device are represented using classes and generalization within a UML Class diagram. A visual domain modeling for IoT based on UML is presented in [7]; it is understandable by users, and it represents logic rules as methods of UML classes. Noticeably, all the works described above do not explicitly associate intelligent rules neither to specific data collected, nor to sensing and sending operations; thus, the *state-dependent behavior* requirements is not met.

As to the *data-centric representation* requirement, the problem of having alternative data representations coexist has been framed as *multi-representation data*. In the context of spatial databases, multi-representation has been proposed [4,16] to assign multiple attributes with different types to the same geographic element, according to the spatial scale used by the system. In the context of database design, multi-representation has been used to take into account temporal and thematic features. For instance, in [16] the MADS model is proposed, where each element of the database schema is annotated with a *stamp* defining a particular representation of the data by the end-user that is associated to some specific rules. This proposal comes with some limitations if used for smart IoT, mainly, methods describing sensing, sending, and transformations are not supported. The usage of UML for multiscale database schemata is proposed in [4], where different types are associated to one geometrical attribute of a class and a class operation is used to change the attribute type according to the scale in input. All these works provide good frameworks to design data with multiple representations but they are not suited for IoT data and their dynamic aspects.

4   A UML Profile for Smart IoT

UML provides a formal extension mechanism through *profiles*, i.e., meta-models that define specialized semantics and rules while respecting the standard UML structure and constraints [11]. The new semantics introduced by a profile allows UML to be customized for specific domains or platforms by extending its metaclasses (e.g., Class, Property, and Package) through Stereotypes, Tagged Values, and OCL constraints.

The STS4IoT UML profile [14] represents IoT applications involving multiple devices which execute different transformations. It can model raw or transformed data according to the application requirements, providing three kinds of operations (aggregation, conversion, and filter) which can be executed at different levels of the IoT network depending on the requirements expressed on data and device capacity. STS4IoT follows the MDA principles by providing an abstract data design (Platform Independent Model - PIM), an implementation view of the data for a specific IoT device (Platform Specific Model - PSM), and an automatic implementation for the selected device (Model-to-Code); thus, it supports

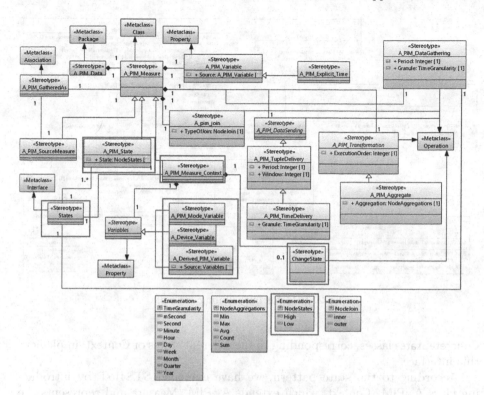

Fig. 1. The SmartSTS4IoT PIM Profile

fast prototyping. The STS4IoT PIM is centered around the A_PIM_Measure class, which represents the data collected by the IoT device. Its attributes (A_PIM_Variable) are the sensed and sent values. A_PIM_Measure comes with two methods representing the sensing and the sending policies: A_PIM_Sensor-Gathering and A_PIM_DataSending, respectively. The original meta-model is shown in Fig. 1; despite its advantages, the STS4IoT approach only supports static data, so it does not take the capabilities of smart IoT into account.

The new elements introduced in our extension of the STS4IoT PIM meta-model, called SmartSTS4IoT, are presented inside red squares in Fig. 1 (the PSM and the device model are not discussed for space reasons). To cope with the requirements related to state-dependent behavior, we adopt the well-known *state pattern*, a behavioral software design pattern that allows an object to change its behavior when its internal state changes [8]. Its UML implementation is based on the Class element; its goal is to make the implementation of the dynamical behavior of class objects transparent and improve maintainability, so that new states can be easily added. It is structured as follows: (i) a Context class is introduced to represent all state-independent data; (ii) Context is associated to a State interface that provides the operations for handling dynamics; (iii) multiple

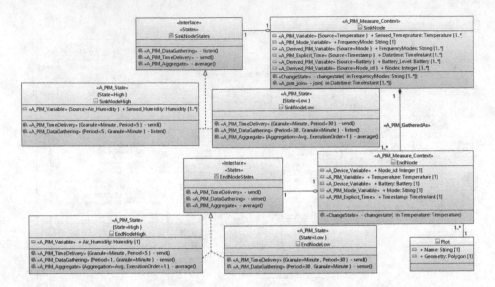

Fig. 2. PIM for our running example

ConcreteState classes, corresponding to the different states of Context, implement this interface.

According to the state pattern, we have extended STS4IoT by introducing class A_PIM_Context, which extends A_PIM_Measure and represents the IoT device data independently from their states and behaviors. A_PIM_Context includes a new operation, ChangeState, in charge of changing states. The device can also send other types of information beside the gathered data, such as internal parameters (represented with the A_Device_Variable stereotype) or data calculated by the device (with the A_Derived_PIM_Variable stereotype).

An example is shown in Fig. 2 to describe the case study of Sect. 2. The EndNode class represents temperature sensors (A_PIM_Variable), which also send a timestamp and the battery level (A_Device_Variable). This class includes the ChangeState operation, which takes in input the temperature value and changes the acquisition and sending policies accordingly. The interface of the state pattern, represented with the States stereotype, is associated to one A_PIM_DataGathering operation and one A_PIM_DataSending operation. Each state is represented with the A_PIM_State class stereotype, which provides a State tagged value to specify the representation currently adopted by the device. Its values (e.g., High and Low) are taken from the NodeStates enumeration.

In our example, the EndNode context class is associated via the EndNodeStates interface to two classes stereotyped A_PIM_State: EndNodeLow and EndNodeHigh. The former represents the behavior of the sensor in the context of a low temperature; in this situation, the sensor senses and sends data every 30 min. Class EndNodeHigh represents the sensor operation when the temperature is high. In this case the sensor is required to sense data every minute, and to send their average every 5 min. Moreover, when in this mode, the device also gathers air humidity data. All EndNodes send their data to SinkNode, which receives the gathered temperature from all the sensors, their battery levels, and their current States. SinkNode changes its state, represented with the stereotype A_Derived_PIM_Variable, according to those of the Endnodes, yielding two possible behaviors: SinkNodeHigh (when all Endnodes are in High mode) and SinkNodeLow (when at least one EndNode is in Low mode). State switching is ruled by ChangeState(), which takes in input the states sent from the EndNodes.

The example described above shows how our UML profile supports the requirements listed in Sect. 2, namely, *internal parameters* and *state-dependent behavior*, by means of a single Class diagram, as requested by the *data-centric representation* requirement.

5 Evaluation and Conclusion

IoT technologies are mature enough to be applied in real-life applications; however, the design and implementation of smart IoT data-centric applications is still time-consuming. In this paper, we have focused on the conceptual design of smart IoT data. We have extended the STS4IoT UML profile for IoT by adapting the state pattern design pattern to allow representing internal parameters as well as dynamic and multi-representation data, which characterize smart IoT. Our SmartSTS4IoT profile comes with all the advantages offered by the state pattern for embedded applications [6], since it separates the different data sensing/sending policies in different classes, thus enabling end-users to focus on one system state at a time, eventually making the UML diagram better readable.

To give a theoretical validation of SmartSTS4IoT we adopted the framework proposed in [3,12], which evaluates a given meta-model again'st 2500 other meta-models in the literature using five quality metrics, namely, *reusability*, *understandability*, *functionality*, *extendibility*, and *well-structuredness*. These metrics are computed by counting some types of elements (e.g., abstract classes, associations, etc.) in the meta-model. It turned out that SmartSTS4IoT has the same quality than STS4IoT in terms of reusability, understandability, functionality, and well-structuredness, while leading to a 163% increase in terms of extendibility (0.29 against 0.11), meaning that new elements can easily be added to our meta-model. We also made a proof-of-concept implementation of our proposal, not described here for lack of space, through a laboratory implementation using the RIOT sensors available in the FIT IoT-LAB testbed [1,2].

We are currently working on the automatic implementation of code for the RIOT platform, aimed at providing a set of large scale experiments to evaluate the conceptual and implementation gains ensured by the SmartSTS4IoT profile.

Acknowledgement. This work has been supported by the French National Research Agency under the IDEX-ISITE Project, initiative 16-IDEX-0001 (CAP 20-25) and by the European Union Next-GenerationEU (PNRR - MISSIONE 4 COMPONENTE 2,

INVESTIMENTO 1.4 - D.D. 1032 17/06/2022, CN00000022). This manuscript reflects only the authors' views and opinions, neither the European Union nor the European Commission can be considered responsible for them.

References

1. Adjih, C., et al.: FIT IoT-LAB: a large scale open experimental IoT testbed. In: Proceedings WF-IoT, Milan, Italy, pp. 459–464 (2015)
2. Baccelli, E., et al.: RIOT: an open source operating system for low-end embedded devices in the IoT. IEEE Internet Things J. **5**(6), 4428–4440 (2018)
3. Basciani, F., Di Rocco, J., Di Ruscio, D., Iovino, L., Pierantonio, A.: A tool-supported approach for assessing the quality of modeling artifacts. J. Comput. Lang. **51**, 173–192 (2019)
4. Bédard, Y., Larrivée, S.: Spatial database modeling with pictrogrammic languages. In: Encyclopedia of GIS, pp. 716–725. Springer, Heidelberg (2008)
5. Bhatnagar, V., Singh, G., Kumar, G., Gupta, R.: Internet of things in smart agriculture: applications and open challenges. Int. J. Students' Res. Technol. Manag. **8**(1), 11–17 (2020)
6. Douglass, B.P.: Design Patterns for Embedded Systems in C: An Embedded Software Engineering Toolkit. Elsevier, Amsterdam (2010)
7. Eterovic, T., Kaljic, E., Donko, D., Salihbegovic, A., Ribic, S.: An internet of things visual domain specific modeling language based on UML. In: Proceedings ICAT, pp. 1–5 (2015)
8. Gamma, E., Helm, R., Johnson, R.E., Vlissides, J.: Design Patterns: Elements of Reusable Object-Oriented Software. Addison-Wesley Professional Computing Series, Addison-Wesley, Reading (1995)
9. Kaur, K., Sharma, A.: Interoperability among internet of things (IoT) components using model-driven architecture approach. In: Proceedings ICTCS, pp. 519–534 (2019)
10. Larrucea, X., Combelles, A., Favaro, J., Taneja, K.: Software engineering for the internet of things. IEEE Softw. **34**(1), 24–28 (2017)
11. Luján-Mora, S., Trujillo, J., Song, I.: A UML profile for multidimensional modeling in data warehouses. Data Knowl. Eng. **59**(3), 725–769 (2006)
12. Ma, Z., He, X., Liu, C.: Assessing the quality of metamodels. Front. Comput. Sci. **7**(4), 558–570 (2013)
13. Patnaik, K.S., Snigdh, I.: Architectural modelling of cyber physical systems using UML. Int. J. Cyber-Phys. Syst. **1**(2), 1–19 (2019)
14. Plazas, J.E., et al.: Sense, transform & send for the internet of things (STS4IoT): UML profile for data-centric IoT applications. Data Knowl. Eng. **139**, 1–29 (2022)
15. Prehofer, C., Chiarabini, L.: From internet of things mashups to model-based development. In: Proceedings COMPSAC, Taichung, Taiwan, pp. 499–504 (2015)
16. Spaccapietra, S., Parent, C., Zimányi, E.: Spatio-temporal and multi-representation modeling: a contribution to active conceptual modeling. In: Proceedings ACM-L Workshop, Tucson, Arizona, pp. 194–205 (2006)
17. Sriram, R.D., Sheth, A.: Internet of things perspectives. IT Prof. **17**(3), 60–63 (2015)

An End-to-End Approach for Online Decision Mining and Decision Drift Analysis in Process-Aware Information Systems

Beate Scheibel[1,2]([✉]) [iD] and Stefanie Rinderle-Ma[3] [iD]

[1] Faculty of Computer Science, Research Group Workflow Systems and Technology,
University of Vienna, Vienna, Austria
`beate.scheibel@univie.ac.at`
[2] UniVie Doctoral School Computer Science DoCS, University of Vienna,
Vienna, Austria
[3] TUM School of Computation, Information and Technology, Technical University
of Munich, Garching, Germany
`stefanie.rinderle-ma@tum.de`

Abstract. Decision mining enables the discovery of decision rules from event logs or streams, and constitutes an important part of in-depth analysis and optimisation of business processes. So far, decision mining has been merely applied in an ex-post way resulting in a snapshot of decision rules for the given chunk of log data. Online decision mining, by contrast, enables continuous monitoring of decision rule evolution and decision drift. Hence this paper presents an end-to-end approach for discovery as well as monitoring of decision points and the corresponding decision rules during runtime, bridging the gap between online control flow discovery and decision mining. The approach is evaluated for feasibility and applicability on four synthetic and one real-life data set.

1 Introduction

Process mining and specifically decision mining allows for increased transparency of processes, which is crucial across all domains [6]. Decision mining is a part of process discovery, allowing for the discovery of decision points (DPs) in a process model and the corresponding decision rules (DRs) guarding that decision based on data elements [4,10]. Decision mining can be seen as a classification problem. Therefore the potential branches that can be chosen and executed are regarded as decision classes. Existing decision mining methods [4] are applied in an ex-post manner. However, when aiming at increased transparency, runtime analysis is particularly interesting, as information about decisions can be communicated to the user in almost real-time and allows for the prompt detection of decision drift, i.e., the manifestation of changing DRs and DPs in event logs and streams. Decision drift can occur due to errors or changes in the environment. Detecting drifts is important to ensure correctness and compliance of a process, i.e., assuring that the drift occurred intentionally. This is crucial across domains such

C. Cabanillas and F. Perez (Eds.): CAiSE 2023, LNBIP 477, pp. 17–25, 2023.
https://doi.org/10.1007/978-3-031-34674-3_3

as manufacturing to ensure quality of products or health care to ensure quality of patient care. Our previous work [11] introduced an approach for detecting decision rule changes during runtime. However, the approach has several limitations. It is assumed that DPs are already known. Therefore the approach cannot be used as end-to-end approach. In addition, the definition of decision drift has been limited to changes in DRs, neglecting DP changes.

As running example consider a simplified loan application process depicted in Fig. 1. The process includes one decision point, i.e., whether a normal or extensive check is necessary. The decision depends on data element *amount_loan*. Assume that during process execution changes can occur, e.g., a change in regulation requires an extensive check for any amount greater than 50.000. Other changes might include additional data that becomes available during runtime and can be used to more accurately mine DRs, e.g., a data element *income*, the addition of an additional branch (class) at the existing decision point, e.g., a branch *Simple Check*, or the addition of a new decision point, e.g., a customer is handled differently depending on the result of the assessment.

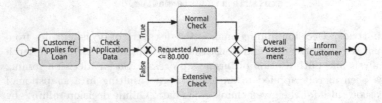

Fig. 1. Running Example, Loan Application

A comprehensive, end-to-end decision mining and monitoring approach should be able to mine and monitor DRs during runtime as soon and as accurately as possible, requiring minimum user input. These requirements can be addressed based on the following questions: RQ1 - What exactly is decision drift and when/why does it happen? RQ2 - How to mine decision points, rules, and drifts in a connected and continuous way without prior knowledge of the process model?

This paper derives and discusses a definition of decision drift and its triggers based on literature ($\mapsto$ RQ1). The approach only requires an event stream as input to provide users with information about DPs, DRs, and potential drifts. The approach is comprehensive as it mines DPs, rules, and drifts in a connected way ($\mapsto$ RQ2). If drift is detected, users are notified to check if these changes are intentional. To account for limited storage and outdated data, a window based approach is taken. Section 2 discusses and defines decision drift concepts. Section 3 describes the approach, which are evaluated in Sect. 4. Related work is discussed in Sect. 5 and a conclusion is provided in Sect. 6.

2   Decision Drift: Definition and Analysis

Decision drift refers to different kinds of changes affecting decisions in a process. A decision is defined by a corresponding decision point in a process model (control flow) and the associated decision rule defining which branch is chosen based on process data (data flow). Decision drift, consequently, can occur due to control flow change, data flow change, and changes to the decision rule itself. Hence, in the following, we analyze state-of-the art approaches for process change (patterns), changes of data and decisions, as well as concept drift, aiming at achieving an understanding and definition of decision drift.

Weber et al. [15] provide a framework of process change patterns referred to as adaptation patterns (AP). The following APs are relevant for decision drift: insertion of process fragments (AP1), including a conditional insert, i.e., an activity is inserted into a process model together with a decision point; deletion of a process fragment (AP2), thereby removing a decision point; addition of a loop (AP8), including the addition of a decision point; addition of a decision point (AP10) and modifications of decision rules (AP13). Hasic et al. [5] define change patterns in Decision Model and Notation (DMN) models and propose four change categories. First, change within decision rules, i.e., including or deleting input or output, or a change in the decision logic. Second, change on decision rules in their entirety, i.e., the inclusion or exclusion of a decision rule from a decision table. Third, change of the decision nodes in the decision requirement diagram (DRD), i.e., deleting/adding a decision node (consisting of multiple decision rules). And lastly, change of the input data nodes in the DRD, i.e., including or excluding data as input. Summarizing the literature , decision changes in a process can potentially include the addition/deletion of: conditions in a decision rule, data elements in a decision rule, decision classes in a decision rule, and decision points in a process model as well as changes of data values in a condition.

Concept drift [2] describes changes in processes with regards to their manifestations in the process execution (logs), i.e., sudden, recurring, gradual, and incremental drift. Accordingly, decision drift can be understood as manifestation of decision changes in process execution logs (ex post) or event streams (online). Decision drifts can be further classified in changes of decision rules (incorporating changes in conditions), decision classes, and decision points. A significant drop in accuracy when predicting newly incoming instances can be seen as sign that decision drift occurred [11]. Changes in decision rules can also be detected by monitoring the branching frequency, i.e., how often a specific branch is chosen [7]. Furthermore, changes in data values can be used to determine if a concept drift occurred [14]. Overall, decision drift can be detected based on (1) decreased performance, (2) changing branching frequency and (3) changes in data elements or data ranges. A comprehensive decision drift analysis approach should be able to monitor occurrence of (1)–(3) in order to detect decision drift.

3   End-to-End Runtime Decision Mining, Monitoring, and Decision Drift Detection Approach

The overall approach is depicted in Fig. 2. The input is an event stream, emitted by, e.g., a process aware information system (PAIS), which is used to mine a process model using online process discovery methods (for an overview of online methods see [3]). The process models are the basis for determining the DPs,

which, in turn, are the basis to mine DRs. The DRs are continuously monitored, using newly incoming events. If either the performance, frequency of taken
branches, or data ranges change, we assume that decision drift occurred and remining is performed. Therefore the approach consists of two continuous processes:
first, the process discovery part continues considering newly occurring events and
remining the process model if necessary. If this leads to new or changed DPs, DRs
are remined as well. Second, the existing DRs are continually checked for compliance with newly incoming events and remined if necessary. A detailed explanation
of the approach can be found in the technical report [12].

The approach works as follows: as soon
as a new event occurs it is stored in a
queue, which continues to store incoming events, while the next phases of the
approach are executed. In addition to
the event stream, the initial grace period
is needed as input, either set manually,
according to the complexity of the underlying DRs and the frequency of new events,
or a default grace period of 200 instances is
used. Each new event is stored as part of a
directly-follows-graph, which contains two
events and the count of how often this combination occurred. *Lossy counting* and the
S-BAR method [17] are used, which continually drop less frequent combinations,
thereby accounting for finite storage and

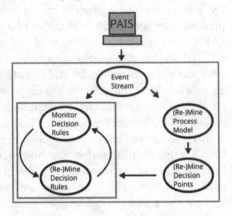

Fig. 2. End-to-End Approach

concept drift. Next, **(Re-)Mine Process Model**, is realized with the Heuristics Miner (HM) [16] using the directly-follows-graph as input. As output, a
petri net is generated, which is used as input for **(Re-)Mine Decision Points**.
Using the algorithm proposed in [10], decision points, i.e., places with multiple outgoing arcs, as well as the decision classes, i.e., the next events, are discovered. A decision point could look like this: *"Check application data"* :
[*"NormalCheck"*, *"ExtensiveCheck"*], i.e. the event before the decision as well
as the decision classes are specified.

After the grace period finishes and DPs have been found, **(Re-)Mine Decision Rules** is performed. Any decision mining method can be applied. Here, a
CART decision tree is used. The mined rules for each decision point are stored
together with the current decision tree models as well as some statistics, for example the accuracy, that will be added during monitoring. In addition, a new ADWIN
instance is generated for the average accuracy, each decision class, and each data
element that is part of the associated decision point. ADWIN is a well-known approach for concept drift detection [1], where the window size is adapted according
to the change of data in the window. ADWIN is used during monitoring to detect
changes.

For each newly occurring event that reflects a decision point, the **Monitor
Decision Rules** function is called, which builds on our previous work presented
in [11] and has been significantly extended and adapted. Instead of relying on

changes in the performance of DRs, monitoring also includes, data elements, i.e. new data elements occurred at a decision point, ranges of data values changed or changes in the branching frequency. Branching frequency refers to the frequency that a decision class, i.e. branch, is chosen and has been shown to indicate changes in underlying decision [7]. The names of the current data elements are compared to the data elements that have occurred before at this decision point, e.g., up until the event *Normal Check* the data elements *requested amount* and *age* were logged for this instance. If unseen data elements, e.g., a data element *income*, are discovered, a drift has been detected. Otherwise, the class for the current decision point is predicted and compared to the actual class, to calculate the current accuracy, which is used in the next step to calculate the average accuracy.

The drift detection method ADWIN [1] is employed in order to detect whether a drift has occurred, either in the performance, i.e., the accuracy of the DRs, the data values, or the branching frequency. ADWIN compares statistics between windows to check if these are significantly different, i.e., a drift happened. As setting the window sizes manually is not trivial, the sizes are chosen according to the amount of changes in the data. If the data is stationary, the window is increased to improve accuracy. If drift occurs, the window is decreased. Each time the monitoring function is called, the average decision rule accuracy is calculated as well as the average branching frequency, i.e. which classes are chosen. For the running example, *Extensive Check* is on average performed for 30% and *Normal Check* for 70% of instances, but then the averages change to 40% and 60% respectively, which could be a sign of decision drift. In addition, the average value for all data elements are calculated, e.g. the average *requested amount* could be 45.000. The calculated averages are used as input to the ADWIN models, which then calculate whether a drift occurred. If a drift is detected, a new decision model is mined and all previous data (averages) and ADWIN models are reset. The ADWIN window size from the model where drift was detected is set as new window size controlling the maximum size of storage, i.e., if the new window size is, for example 500, no more than 500 instances are stored for that decision point. This allows to dynamically adapt the amount of instances stored, which is necessary as storage is limited and only recent data should be used for remining.

4   Evaluation

The approach was implemented using python and is available online[1]. The BPIC17 log is used for evaluating the applicability of the approach. In order to show its feasibility, we use four synthetic data sets (SD).

Feasability - Synthetic Datasets: SD I–IV are based on the running example depicted in Fig. 1 and contain the following decision drifts: I) value changes in a condition, II) additional data elements in a decision rule, III) additional branch for a decision point and IV) an additional decision point. The datasets, consisting of 5000 instances each, have been created using random variations and are stored in a queue (event by event) in order to simulate an event stream.

---

[1] https://github.com/bscheibel/dmma-e

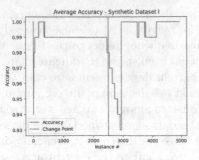

(a) SD I: Decision Rule Change.

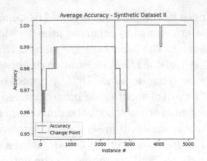

(b) SD II: Decision Rule Change.

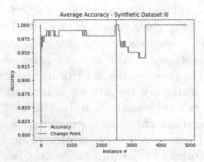

(c) SD III: Decision Class Change.

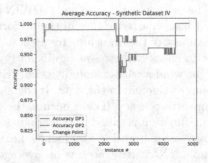

(d) SD IV: Decision Point Change.

Fig. 3. Evaluation of SD I-IV.

SD I–IV together with the complete evaluation results, including all DRs, are available online[3] and show that the mined rules are equal to the underlying rules. The results can be seen in Fig. 3. For each SD the accuracy decreased significantly after the change. As soon as the rules were remined, the accuracy increased again. Figure 3d shows that the additional DP was discovered quickly and an additional remine was performed later on to achieve higher accuracy.

Applicability - BPIC17: The BPIC17 data set[2] consists of a loan application process. Pre-processing was done to simulate an event stream.

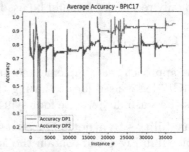

The process model was remined throughout the process: in the beginning it contained one DP, then a second one was discovered as can be seen in Fig. 4. For example, the last mined rule for DP2, i.e., if the offer was accepted, contains the condition that the offer is accepted if the CreditScore is above 324. The exact values in the decisions change with each remining. This and the frequent remining is probably due

Fig. 4. BPIC17 Results.

[2] https://data.4tu.nl/articles/dataset/BPI_Challenge_2017/12696884.

to insufficient data, i.e. not all data elements that the decision is based on, is part of the event log.

4.1 Discussion

RQ1 is addressed in Sect. 2 by defining decision drift as changes in decision rules, decision classes, and decision points. **RQ2** is answered by providing an end-to-end approach that does not require the user to specify the DPs beforehand and continually monitors the performance, branching frequency as well as data values for changes to detect drift. To deal with limited storage and outdated data, an adaptive window technique is used (ADWIN). The evaluation of the synthetic datasets shows that the approach is feasible and able to discover different kinds of decision drift. For the real-life dataset, the evaluation shows that the approach is able to work with real-life data. In terms of interpretability, the output consists of textual DRs, which enables manual interpretation and analysis. To further optimize the approach, decision trees that are optimized for runtime classification, e.g. Incremental Decision Trees [8], could be used. However, these algorithms continually adapt the rules to achieve the best performance, without the necessity of underlying changes. Exploring the meaningful application will be part of future work. **Limitations:** So far only sudden drifts have been studied and no time complexity analysis was done. Further evaluations on more complex real life datasets are necessary to show the generalisability of the approach.

5 Related Work

The first decision mining approach [10] includes an algorithm for detecting DPs from a Petri Net as well as classification techniques to mine the DRs. Subsequent approaches focus on specific aspects of decision mining (for an overview see [4]), employing ex-post algorithms. Recently, online or runtime analysis is gaining traction for online process discovery [9] and drift detection [13]. Drift detection, partly overlaps with decision drift analysis as changes in DPs are part of control flow drift. None of these approaches include decision drift analysis, the remining of DPs and rules, and the textual generation of DRs. [7] propose a method for identifying decision rule changes based on changes in the branching frequency. This is done ex-post and neither DP discovery nor remining are part of the approach. This work constitutes a significant extension of our previous work [11] where it was assumed that DPs already known and no changes of DPs occur.

6 Conclusion

This paper presents an end-to-end approach for mining decision rules during runtime, as well as monitoring of decision drift, and updating decision points and the associated rules if necessary. The output comprises textual decision rules for each discovered decision point, that are updated as soon as decision drift is detected, as support for users to evaluate if these changes are intentional, enabling increased transparency. The evaluation shows that the approach is able to detect different kinds of decision drift with high accuracy and to work with real-life data. However, further testing is planned for future work.

Acknowledgements. This work has been partly supported and funded by the Austrian Research Promotion Agency (FFG) via the Austrian Competence Center for Digital Production (CDP) under the contract number 881843 and the Deutsche Forschungsgemeinschaft (DFG, German Research Foundation) – project number 277991500.

References

1. Bifet, A., Gavaldà, R.: Learning from time-changing data with adaptive windowing. In: SIAM International Conference on Data Mining, pp. 443–448 (2007)
2. Bose, R.P.J.C., van der Aalst, W.M.P., Zliobaite, I., Pechenizkiy, M.: Dealing with concept drifts in process mining. IEEE Trans. Neural Networks Learn. Syst. **25**(1), 154–171 (2014)
3. Burattin, A.: Streaming process mining. In: van der Aalst, W.M.P., Carmona, J. (eds.) Process Mining Handbook, pp. 349–372. Springer, Cham (2022). https://doi.org/10.1007/978-3-031-08848-3_11
4. de Leoni, M., Mannhardt, F.: Decision discovery in business processes. In: Encyclopedia of Big Data Technologies, pp. 1–12 (2018)
5. Hasić, F., Corea, C., Blatt, J., Delfmann, P., Serral, E.: Decision model change patterns for dynamic system evolution. Knowl. Inf. Syst. **62**(9), 3665–3696 (2020). https://doi.org/10.1007/s10115-020-01469-w
6. Leewis, S., Berkhout, M., Smit, K.: Future challenges in decision mining at governmental institutions. In: Americas Conference on Information Systems, p. 12 (2020)
7. Lu, Y., Chen, Q., Poon, S.K.: Detecting and understanding branching frequency changes in process models (2021)
8. Manapragada, C., Webb, G.I., Salehi, M.: Extremely fast decision tree. In: PKnowledge Discovery & Data Mining, pp. 1953–1962 (2018)
9. Navarin, N., Cambiaso, M., Burattin, A., Maggi, F.M., Oneto, L., Sperduti, A.: Towards online discovery of data-aware declarative process models from event streams. In: Neural Networks, pp. 1–8 (2020)
10. Rozinat, A., van der Aalst, W.M.P.: Decision mining in ProM. In: Business Process Management, pp. 420–425 (2006)
11. Scheibel, B., Rinderle-Ma, S.: Online decision mining and monitoring in process-aware information systems. In: Conceptual Modeling, pp. 271–280 (2022)
12. Scheibel, B., Rinderle-Ma, S.: An end-to-end approach for online decision mining and decision drift analysis in process-aware information systems: Extended Version (2023). https://arxiv.org/abs/2303.03961
13. Stertz, F., Rinderle-Ma, S.: Process histories - detecting and representing concept drifts based on event streams. In: OTM Conferences, pp. 318–335 (2018)
14. Stertz, F., Rinderle-Ma, S.: Detecting and identifying data drifts in process event streams based on process histories. In: CAiSE Forum, pp. 240–252 (2019)
15. Weber, B., Reichert, M., Rinderle-Ma, S.: Change patterns and change support features - enhancing flexibility in process-aware information systems. Data Knowl. Eng. **66**(3), 438–466 (2008)

16. Weijters, A.J.M.M., Ribeiro, J.T.S.: Flexible heuristics miner (FHM). In: Computational Intelligence and Data Mining, pp. 310–317 (2011)
17. van Zelst, S.J., van Dongen, B.F., van der Aalst, W.M.P.: Event stream-based process discovery using abstract representations. Knowl. Inf. Syst. 54(2), 407–435 (2018)

Towards Designing Energy-Aware Cybersecurity Policies

Mattia Salnitri[1(✉)], Pierluigi Plebani[1], and Alessandra Raffone[2]

[1] Politecnico di Milano, Milan, Italy
{mattia.salnitri,pierluigi.plebani}@polimi.it
[2] AlmavivA S.p.A., Rome, Italy
a.raffone@almaviva.it

Abstract. Cybersecurity is a fundamental aspect of socio-technical systems. Unfortunately, the price to pay for a secure system is an overhead of computational power and, therefore, of energy consumption. With the last global events, energy consumption is not anymore a secondary effect but should become a relevant driver of decisions on the security measures to implement. Thus, the design of security policies for socio-technical systems should consider energy consumption to carefully choose security measures to deploy. Security policies identify the security objectives of actors in socio-technical systems, the security measures that enforce them, and the business processes affected by these measures. In this direction, the goal of this paper is to propose a method for the energy-aware design of security policies. An estimation of the energy consumption of security goals will be calculated to allow the definition of security policies considering their energy consumption.

Keywords: Security policy · Energy consumption

1 Introduction

Cybersecurity is a fundamental aspect of every socio-technical systems. Due to the extreme importance and interest in cybersecurity, other aspects such as energy consumption, have usually been considered negligible. More recently, this trend is changing and with the last global extreme climate and geopolitical events, energy consumption is gaining more and more relevance and many companies are increasingly considering strategies to reduce energy consumption.

Among those strategies, also cybersecurity is considered liable of a relevant part of IT consumption [9]. Following the same rationale of the security-by-design principle, the sooner the energy consumption of cybersecurity is considered in the design of socio-technical systems, the higher the positive impact on energy saving. In this context, security policies hold a central role. In fact, these documents are the result of the design phase and they delineate the overall approach to the security of organizations.

The goal of this paper is to introduce a method that guides the energy-aware design of security policies for socio-technical systems. The method will

C. Cabanillas and F. Perez (Eds.): CAiSE 2023, LNBIP 477, pp. 26–33, 2023.
https://doi.org/10.1007/978-3-031-34674-3_4

help reduce energy consumption and cost of the overall socio-technical system while contributing to the goals of green computing [8]. Unfortunately, to the best of our knowledge, in the state of the art, no method or solution is proposed for such an ambitious goal. The proposed method includes two graphical modeling languages to define security policies and their related energy consumption.

The paper is structured as follows. Section 2 defines the conceptual levels that shape the method proposed in this paper, while Sect. 3 describes the modeling languages, the relation between them and energy consumption propagation. Section 4 describes the measurement of energy consumption of security measures. Section 5 shows the related work and Sect. 6 concludes the paper.

2 Energy-aware Design Method

Security policies are the statement of top management intent on how to protect socio-technical systems and ensure the security and privacy of sensitive data. Security policies are materialized in documents that describe the directions, responsibilities, and technical security solutions to achieve their mission.

The proposed method approaches security policies by dividing them in three conceptual levels, shown in Fig. 1, each of them addressing different aspects of security of socio-technical systems. The first level addresses *security goals*, i.e., the security-related objectives of each actor involved in the system. The second level defines the *security measures*, such as encryption algorithms or firewalls, that are deployed and used in the systems. The third level consists of *business processes* that are executed in the system, where security measures are deployed.

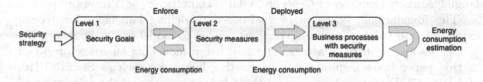

Fig. 1. Conceptualization of security policies in three layers

The method proposed in this paper aims at modelling all conceptual levels, the first two to specify security policies, while the third one to specify how security measures are deployed and used, and to estimate their energy consumption. This information is propagated back to security goals to allow security experts to take proper design choices to reduce energy consumption of security policies.

3 Modeling Conceptual Levels

In order to specify the concepts required at each conceptual level defined in Sect. 2, we propose two graphical modelling languages. A goal-based modelling language for the first two levels and one for business processes for the third level.

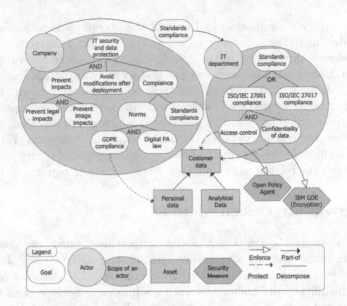

Fig. 2. Example of a security policy modelled with the goal-based language proposed.

3.1   Goal Based Modelling Language

Goal-based modeling languages are graphical modelling languages centered on the notion of goal [1,15], that represents an objective that can be achieved. The top part of Fig. 2 shows a diagram obtained using a goal-based modelling language, where examples of *Goals* are "GDPR compliance" or "Prevent impacts".

The foundational concepts of goal-based modelling languages have been extended with the concepts and relations needed to model energy consumption properties and security measures. The goal based modelling language proposed in this paper takes inspiration from existing languages such as SecTRO [10] and BIM [7]. Unfortunately, none of these languages have all the relations and concepts needed, while including other ones that are not relevant for this paper.

We included the elements of goal-based modelling languages as goal, goal decomposition, actor and delegation, and included the following security concepts.

– **Security measure**: it represents a method that enforce security goals. This concept is based on the concept of security mechanism of SecTRO.
– **Asset**: it represents any valuable resource for socio-technical systems, e.g., a piece of data, a data source, a physical computing node, etc. Figure 2 shows three assets: "Customer data", "Personal data" and "Analytical data".

The following relations are included.

– **Enforce(Goal → Security Measure)**: it specifies that a security measure will satisfy a security goal. This is based on the relation between Goal and

Plan in TROPOS [1] or Goal and Task in BIM [7]. For example, in Fig. 2 "OPA for data" security measure enforces the security goal "Access control provisioned". Only one security measure can be linked to a security goal.

- **Protect(Goal → Asset)**: it specifies that a security goal aims to protect an asset. For example, in Fig. 2 "Access control provisioned" security goal protects the asset "Customer data". Only one goal can be linked to an asset.
- **Part-of(Asset → Asset)**: it allows to specify that an asset is part of another asset, following the Mereology approach [3]. For example, in Fig. 2 "Personal Data" and "Analytical data" are part of "Customer data" asset.
- **Is-A(Security measure → Security measure)**: it allows to model specific instances of the same security measure. For example, in Fig. 2 "Open Policy Agent" is linked to "OPA for data" and "OPA for function access"

The modelling language proposed uses the well-known concepts of goal-based research field and security to specify cybersecurity policies. It allows modelling security goals of actors identifying, therefore, the security responsibilities within the system. Each security goals can then be linked to one or more assets it needs to protect and to the security measure(s) that will be deployed to enforce the goals and, therefore, protect the assets.

The estimation of energy consumption of security measures will be calculated using the third conceptual layer. Following the *Protect* relations, the energy consumed to protect an asset can be determined, while following the *Enforce* relations and the *goal decomposition*, the energy consumption of security goals can be estimated. To support this analysis, the modelling language is further extended with a property that specifies the energy consumption, on all concepts.

These rules allow to estimate energy consumption of security goals and assets, allowing to evaluate the best security strategy to reduce energy consumption.

3.2   Business Process Modelling Language

This paper uses business processes to estimate energy consumption of security measures. We chose business processes since they represent the know-how of socio-technical systems, i.e., they model how systems achieve their objectives.

To achieve the aim of this paper, business processes modelled for the method need to include information on the security measures, specified with the modelling language defined in the previous subsection. Furthermore, to estimate energy consumption, information related to the execution frequency and amount of data that are feed to security measures need to be specified in the model.

The most used modelling notation for business process is BPMN 2.0 [11]. Yet, this modelling language does not include all properties required. We, therefore, extend the modelling language with the following properties: (i) security measures deployed in the process; (ii) frequency of execution on business process; (iii) size of data object representing data sets.

The following BPMN elements are extended with the properties listed before, while Fig. 3 shows an example of a BPMN diagram extended the properties.

- Business process: the frequency of execution of the process is included and may be specified, if known. The top part of Fig. 3 shows an example of an extended BPMN diagram with the frequency of execution reported. For each exclusive, inclusive or event based gateway a distribution of probability of execution of outgoing control flows will need to be provided.

- Task: the security measure(s) that are activated and an estimation of their energy consumption can be specified.
- Data object: the security measure(s) that are activated when the data object is used. If the data object is an electronic document, information on its size will be included. An estimation of energy consumed can be specified.
- Message flow: the security measure(s) that are activated when the message flow is activated. If the message exchanges an electronic document, its size will be included. An estimation of energy consumed may be specified.

These properties, allow to determine how much security measures will be executed, on which task/data. With this information and knowing the energy consumption of security measure, it is possible to estimate the overall energy consumption of a security measure within a process.

If it is possible to estimate the energy consumption based on element execution, the information will be added on the property of the element. If it is possible to estimate the energy consumption per business process execution, the information will be added on the property of the business process. If it is only possible to estimate the energy consumption of the security measure as a whole, then this information will be specified on the security measure in the goal model.

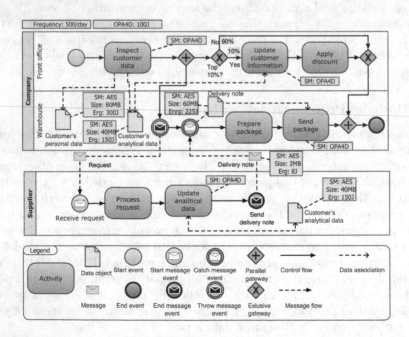

Fig. 3. Example of a business process modeled with the proposed modelling language.

Table 1. Cardinatility of mapping relations

Goal-based concept	Card.		Business process concept
	→	←	
Security measure	0:N	1:1	Security measure
Asset	0:N	0:N	Data object
Asset	0:N	0:N	Message

Table 2. Example of mapping relations

Goal-based con.	Business process con.
Personal data	Customer's personal data
Personal data	Delivery note
Analytical data	Customer's analytical data
OPA for data	OPA4D
AES	AES

3.3 Mapping Concepts

To support the propagation of energy consumption calculated in business processes to the security goals of the modelling language, we define a conceptual map between concepts of the two languages.

We linked the concept of *Security measure* of the goal-based modelling language with the same concept of the business process language. This map allows to propagate energy consumption, if present, from the business process concept to the goal model one. The propagated values are the overall consumption estimated per process. We also mapped *Asset* with *Data object* and *Message*.

Table 1 shows the mapping of concepts with the cardinality, while Table 2 shows the mapping between concepts of diagrams shown in Figs. 2 and 3. "OPA for Data" is mapped to "OPA4D", that is the OPA implementation. The "4D" part is added on the business process for mapping readability.

4 Energy Consumption of Security Measures

As described in Sect. 3, energy consumption estimation of security goals is derived from the consumption of the security measures deployed in the analyzed socio-technical system and linked to elements in the modelled business processes.

Energy consumption calculation or measurement in some research fields, such as IoT, is a well-established practice. This allows to have a knowledge based of energy consumption of some security measure, unluckily, for many new technologies energy consumption information is not provided and needs to be measured after the system is deployed. Fortunately, there exists software tools that measure energy consumption. For example, Android offers APIs to measure energy consumption, while software tools such as Intel Power gadget or Nvidia-SMI use hardware APIs to monitor energy consumption. With these software tools, it is possible to calculate energy consumption of a node with and without an active security mechanism and calculate its energy consumption.

5 Related Work

This research work is built on top of two main pillars: the relationship between security and energy consumption and the modeling of this relationship.

Concerning the first aspect, few research work addressed the relationship between energy consumption and security mechanisms. Most of them have considered this issue in terms of algorithm or software optimization, especially IoT-based environments. Green cybersecurity [2] research area mainly focuses on the reduction of environmental impact of security measures, which is only partially linked with energy consumption. Yet, many of the research work in this research field focus on implementation of energy efficient security measures, without considering the design phase and its impact on energy saving.

We surveyed the state of the art [5,6] but, as far as our knowledge goes, no goal-based modelling language met our expressiveness requirements.

Some goal-based modelling languages, such as Socio-Technical Security [12] and other extension i^* extension oriented to security [5] are focused on modeling the functional goals of actors, not the security ones. Other modelling languages, such as SecTRO (Secure TROPOS) [10] and the one proposed by Elhai and Yu [4], cover the concept of *Security objective* and *Security mechanism*. Secure TROPOS uses the concept of *Threat* and *Security constraint* to connect functional goals with *Security mechanisms*. Unluckily, these research work include concepts such as *Threat*, that are not usually part of security policies, but are described in other documents as the risk analysis documents and, therefore, are out of scope of the method proposed in this paper.

For what concerns the modelling of procedures, the state of the art offers modelling languages that allow to specify security concepts in business processes. Some of them extends BPMN, for example, Rodriguez [13] or SecBPMN2 [14]. Many of these languages include security concepts intended as requirements on the execution of elements of the process. For example, in Rodriguez [13] and SecBPMN2 [14], integrity security concept is modelled as a security annotation linked to a data object, meaning that the platform storing the data object should satisfy the requirement. Frequently, security annotations specify security measures that are used to satisfy the implicitly related requirements, for example encryption can be specified as a security measure to enforce integrity of data.

This paper, however, takes a different approach allowing to specify security objectives on the tree structure of the goal-based modeling language, permitting to organize security objectives and perform analyses. In our case, therefore, it is not anymore necessary to include security requirements in business process models, leaving to specify only security measures and their energy consumption in the model of the processes. This allows a separation of concerns between the management of security objectives and the definition of the deployment of security measures. Unfortunately, as far as our knowledge goes no graphical modelling language allows to specify security mechanisms, their energy consumption and information on the execution of the process.

6   Conclusions

This paper proposes an innovative method for the energy-aware design of security policies of socio-technical systems. The method guides the design of security policies, considering energy consumption as a major selection criteria of security goals to be achieved, and security measures to be adopted. The method has been preliminary tested with real security policies of a company.

Acknowledgment. This project has received funding from the European Union's Horizon Europe under grant agreement no. 101070186 (TEADAL) and by the European Social Fund REACT EU-National Research and Innovation Operational Program 2014–2020, Ministry of University and Research.

References

1. Bresciani, P., Perini, A., Giorgini, P., Giunchiglia, F., Mylopoulos, J.: Tropos: an agent-oriented software development methodology. Auton. Agent. Multi-Agent Syst. **8**(3), 203–236 (2004)
2. Caviglione, L., Merlo, A., Migliardi, M.: What is green security? In: International Conference on Information Assurance and Security (IAS), pp. 366–371. IEEE (2011)
3. Cotnoir, A., Varzi, A.C.: Mereology. Oxford University Press, Oxford (2021)
4. Elahi, G., Yu, E.: A goal oriented approach for modeling and analyzing security trade-offs. In: Parent, C., Schewe, K.-D., Storey, V.C., Thalheim, B. (eds.) ER 2007. LNCS, vol. 4801, pp. 375–390. Springer, Heidelberg (2007). https://doi.org/10.1007/978-3-540-75563-0_26
5. Gonçalves, E., Castro, J., Araújo, J., Heineck, T.: A systematic literature review of istar extensions. J. Syst. Softw. **137**, 1–33 (2018)
6. Horkoff, J., et al.: Goal-oriented requirements engineering: an extended systematic mapping study. Requirements Eng. **24**, 133–160 (2019)
7. Horkoff, J., et al.: Making data meaningful: the business intelligence model and its formal semantics in description logics. In: Meersman, R., et al. (eds.) OTM 2012. LNCS, vol. 7566, pp. 700–717. Springer, Heidelberg (2012). https://doi.org/10.1007/978-3-642-33615-7_17
8. Kurp, P.: Green computing. Commun. ACM **51**(10), 11–13 (2008)
9. Merlo, A., Migliardi, M., Caviglione, L.: A survey on energy-aware security mechanisms. Pervasive Mob. Comput. **24**, 77–90 (2015)
10. Mouratidis, H., Giorgini, P.: Secure tropos: a security-oriented extension of the tropos methodology. Int. J. Softw. Eng. Knowl. Eng. **17**(02), 285–309 (2007)
11. OMG: BPMN 2.0. Technical Report, January 2011. http://www.omg.org/spec/BPMN/2.0
12. Paja, E., Dalpiaz, F., Giorgini, P.: Modelling and reasoning about security requirements in socio-technical systems. Data Knowl. Eng. **98**, 123–143 (2015)
13. Rodríguez, A., Fernández-Medina, E., Piattini, M.: A BPMN extension for the modeling of security requirements in business processes. IEICE Trans. Inf. Syst. **90**(4), 745–752 (2007)
14. Salnitri, M., Paja, E., Giorgini, P.: Maintaining secure business processes in light of socio-technical systems' evolution. In: 2016 IEEE 24th International Requirements Engineering Conference Workshops (REW), pp. 155–164. IEEE (2016)
15. Yu, E.: Modeling strategic relationships for process reengineering. Soc. Model. Requirements Eng. **11**(2011), 66–87 (2011)

A Data-Driven Methodology for Guiding the Selection of Preprocessing Techniques in a Machine Learning Pipeline

Jorge García-Carrasco$^{(\boxtimes)}$ [iD], Alejandro Maté [iD], and Juan Trujillo [iD]

Lucentia Research Group - Department of Software and Computing Systems,
University of Alicante, Ctra. de San Vicente del Raspeig,
s/n, 03690 San Vicente del Raspeig, Spain
jorge.g@ua.es

Abstract. The performance of a Machine Learning (ML) model greatly depends on the previous preprocessing of the data. Unfortunately, the decision on which preprocessing techniques should be applied relies on the expertise of data scientists and/or ML practitioners. Since the correct application of some techniques depend on the characteristics of the data whereas others depend on the particular ML model to be trained, this leads to an error-prone process that requires the data scientist to be knowledgeable in all the combinations that may arise. To tackle this problem, we propose a methodology that guides the selection of the most appropriated preprocessing techniques that are highly required or strongly recommended taking into account both the ML model as well as the data characteristics, so that the developer is able to freely experiment with different models while ensuring that no needed preprocessing techniques are overlooked. According to the ML model and the data at hand, the methodology will (i) obtain the characteristics of the model (ii) check whether these characteristics are met by the data or not and (iii) show to the developer which variables require preprocessing and which techniques should be applied so that a proper decision can be made. To the best of our knowledge, this is the only work that tries to gather the most common ML models together with its most adequate preprocessing techniques and encode this information into a methodology that guides this process in a systematic way.

Keywords: Data-driven · Preprocessing · Methodology · Data Science

1 Introduction

Machine Learning (ML) is a sub-field of Artificial Intelligence (AI) comprised by methods which are able to "learn" from data, i.e. automatically recognize patterns in data which can then be used to perform several tasks such as forecasting, classifying, or predicting among others [5].

The performance of an ML model can greatly depend on the preprocessing of the training data [7,10,18]. The decision on which preprocessing techniques

© The Author(s), under exclusive license to Springer Nature Switzerland AG 2023
C. Cabanillas and F. Perez (Eds.): CAiSE 2023, LNBIP 477, pp. 34–42, 2023.
https://doi.org/10.1007/978-3-031-34674-3_5

should be applied relies on the expertise of the data scientist and/or ML practitioner acting as ML developer. Unfortunately, the correct techniques to apply vary depending on both the data at hand and the particular model being trained, requiring deep expertise of all models and situations that may arise. This is further exacerbated due to the "no free lunch" theorem [19], which states that all optimization models have the same performance when averaging through every possible problem. This implies that there is no global best model and, thus, for each particular problem several ML models -with multiple tailored preprocessing combinations- should be tested in order to find the best performant.

Hence, the current approach to obtain a performant ML pipeline (i.e. the combination of applied preprocessing techniques and ML model) implies experimenting with different preprocessing techniques and ML models via a trial-and-error process. Even though most techniques applied should be supported by the Exploratory Data Analysis (EDA), there are certain techniques whose application depends on the nature of the ML model. In other words, each ML model imposes certain requisites on the input data in order to work well, or even to work at all.

For example, a logistic regression model for classification has better results when the data is normalized and its performance decreases if some input variable follows a skewed distribution or if correlated variables are present. Moreover, it is only able to handle numerical data, thus, the categorical variables must be encoded in order to exploit their information. On the other hand, a decision tree directly supports categorical data and unscaled or skewed data does not particularly hinder its performance. Therefore, this implies that some of the preprocessing techniques (such as centering, standardizing, or applying the Box-Cox transformation to reduce the skewness of a distribution) should be automatically selected due to the type of model to be trained.

This type of knowledge is commonly acquired via the experience of data scientists and ML practitioners across several projects. Unfortunately, it is easy to overlook some of the required preprocessing techniques, even for expert practitioners. For example, even though the autors of [3] successfully developed an ML model to forecast the cancellation of hotel bookings, they mention experimenting with an SVM-based model, which is negatively affected when working with skewed variables. However, there is no mention of applying any preprocessing technique that tries to reduce the skewness on the data, despite the presence of skewed variables. Similarly, the author of [16] developed a model for successfully predicting diabetes mellitus. Despite experimenting with a logistic regression and SVM models, no preprocessing techniques were used to transform the skewed variables present in the training data, which negatively affects these models.

By designing a methodology that encodes this knowledge, (i) the preprocessing step becomes less prone to this type of errors, (ii) the performant model can be obtained faster due to the mandatory preprocessing techniques being covered right from the start of the project and (iii) the practitioner is able to put more effort in other important aspects of the development process, such as trying different models or feature engineering [14].

Therefore, in this paper we propose a methodology that guides the selection of preprocessing techniques that are required or strongly recommended for the type of ML model and data to be used. According to the ML model and the data at hand, the methodology will (i) obtain the characteristics of the model (e.g. its performance is decreased by the presence of correlated or skewed variables, etc.), (ii) check whether these characteristics are met by the data or not (e.g. *var_1* is skewed) and (iii) show to the developer which variables require preprocessing and which set of techniques should be applied (e.g. apply Box-Cox [6] or Yeo-Johnson [20] transform to *var_1*). The methodology will make use of two proposed catalogues, namely the ML models and the preprocessing techniques catalogues, which will be described later.

To the best of our knowledge, this is the only work that tries to gather the most common ML models together with its most adequate preprocessing techniques and encode this information into a methodology that guides this process in a systematic way. We are convinced that our proposal not only will be (i) an excellent resource for beginners, but also (ii) a useful methodology for practitioners that have to tackle a new problem where an ML model should be developed, thereby reducing the probability of error and the time consumed by the most time-consuming step in the process: the preprocessing step. Indeed, the authors of [17] conducted several interviews with data scientists, in which most of them agreed that data preprocessing is one of the most time-consuming and laborious tasks.

The remainder of the paper is structured as follows: Sect. 2 presents the related work, Sect. 3 describes the proposed methodology and its main components, as well as a brief, illustrative example of use and Sect. 4 will provide the conclusions and future work.

2   Related Work

It is widely accepted that the preprocessing of the data is one of the most important and time-consuming steps when developing an ML model. This is because the performance of an ML model is strongly tied to such preprocessing of the data. Many works that assess this impact can be found in literature [7,10,18]. In fact, movements such as Data-centric AI [1] have emerged highlighting the need to focus on the data aspect when developing an ML system rather than focusing solely on the modeling aspect. Unfortunately, as these movements point out, overlooking the data aspect so far has led to a lack of adequate tools, best practices, and infrastructure to manage data in modern ML systems.

Lately, increasing efforts have been put into the field of automatic ML (AutoML) [12]. AutoML aims to reduce human intervention by automatizing the process of designing an ML pipeline for a given task by evaluating different combinations of preprocessing and ML models. Despite not being the main objective, these techniques (e.g. AUTO-SKLEARN [9]) also take into account the automatic selection of preprocessing techniques. While this certainly reduces the burden of choosing the right preprocessing techniques, the goal is not to provide a systematic tool for the proper selection of preprocessing techniques, but to reduce human intervention by automatizing the development of an ML system. Moreover, the temporal and computational cost is increased, as many different pipelines have to be evaluated.

In an effort to improve the overall process of developing ML models, the concept of MLOps [2] has been on the rise recently. MLOps is comprised by a set of practices which aim to ease the deployment and maintenance of ML solutions. Our work is fully aligned with the values of MLOps, as it tries to systematize the process of selecting the correct preprocessing techniques.

As we have seen, there is a clear lack of tools to tackle preprocessing on ML systems, despite being the most time-consuming task. Unfortunately, we think that proposals such as AutoML might not be the most suitable option regarding preprocessing, as reducing human intervention might give undesirable results, whereas the community, aligned with the values of MLOps and Data-centric AI, claims clear and systematic steps to professionalize the development of ML systems.

3   A Data-Driven Methodology for Guiding the Selection of Preprocessing Techniques

As previously mentioned, the objective of the proposed methodology is to guide the selection of preprocessing techniques according to the ML model and data to be used. The required preprocessing techniques will be covered right from the first training iteration, which makes the process less error-prone and time consuming, therefore allowing the developer to focus in other important aspects of developing, such as experimenting with other models and/or feature engineering.

To achieve this goal, the methodology will make use of two catalogues, namely the *ML models catalogue* and the *preprocessing techniques catalogue*. The ML models catalogue contains information about the assumptions that are made on the data for each model. For every model in the catalogue, the following questions are answered:

- Does it require standarized variables?
- Is it affected by correlation?
- Is it affected by skewed variables?
- Does it directly supports categorical variables?
- Does it support missing data?
- Is it robust to outliers?

Essentially, these questions indicate how the model is affected by the characteristics of the data, which eventually derives in which preprocessing techniques have to be applied, as we will present later in this section. For example, a Support Vector Machine (SVM) requires its input data to be standarized and not skewed, it is not affected by correlated data, the categorical variables should be properly encoded, it does not support missing data and it is robust to outliers.

This set of questions was developed according to our experience as ML practitioners in several real-world projects as well as to which where the most important data-related aspects for characterizing a model according to the literature reviewed [5, 14, 15].

On the other hand, the preprocessing techniques catalogue contains tests that are used to check if the data meets the characteristics imposed by the model or not and which preprocessing techniques can be applied in the latter case to improve the situation. For example, the D'Agostino-Pearson K^2 statistic [8] can be used to test whether a variable is skewed or not and, in the case that a variable is skewed, preprocessing techniques such as the Box-Cox [6] or the Yeo-Johnson [20] transforms can be used.

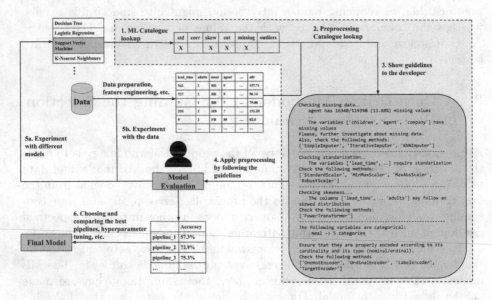

Fig. 1. Diagram that shows the role of the methodology (region inside dashed lines) in the process of developing an ML pipeline.

Figure 1 shows a diagram of how the methodology works and the role that it has in the whole process of developing an ML pipeline. First, the developer selects an ML model and prepares the input data for the model. Then, the following steps are performed:

1. Lookup into the ML catalogue to obtain the characteristics of the ML model. For example, an SVM requires its input data to be standarized and not skewed, the categorical variables should be properly encoded and it does not support missing data.

2. Lookup into the preprocessing techniques catalogue to retrieve which tests can be used to diagnose whether a variable meets the required characteristics or not, and in the latter case, the set of preprocessing techniques that can be applied to each variable.
3. Given the previous information, a set of guidelines are shown to the developer. These guidelines show which variables do not meet the characteristics stated by the model and suggests a set of preprocessing techniques that can be applied to each of these variables. For example, in the case of a SVM, it will show to the user which variables have missing data and which preprocessing techniques can be used to input such missing values, etc.
4. With the aid of these guidelines, the developer applies the right preprocessing techniques so that the data meets the characteristics of the ML model. Then, the developer evaluates the resulting ML pipeline (i.e. the combination of the chosen preprocessing techniques and the ML model).
5. After evaluating the current pipeline, the developer can keep (a) experimenting with different ML models or (b) experimenting with the data i.e. feature engineering (building new variables, discarding variables, data cleaning, etc.). In both cases, it is likely that the required set of preprocessing techniques changes. However, thanks to the guidelines, the developer will always be aware of these changes and will be able to select the adequate preprocessing techniques for the current pipeline.
6. Finally, after experimenting with different combinations, the developer chooses the most suitable pipeline as the final model.

To build the ML models catalogue we performed an extensive review of general ML books [5, 13, 15]. These resources, along several works that focused on specific ML models were used to characterize the most common ML models according to its input data. We covered the most common ML models that we found by reviewing the literature, namely Linear/Logistic Regression with Lasso or Ridge regression, Decision Tree, Support Vector Machine, Naive Bayes, K-Nearest Neighbours and Neural Networks (in its most basic form, i.e. a Multilayer Perceptron). Similarly, the preprocessing catalogue was built after extensively reviewing books related to preprocessing in ML [14, 15] complemented by different specific works. For each characteristic of the data, the catalogue will provide (i) methods to diagnose whether a variable meets a characteristic or not and (ii) which preprocessing techniques can be applied in the latter case. It is important to mention that, even though the diagnosis is mostly automatized, the practitioner should always check or further investigate the data, as the methodology does not aim to fully automatize the process, but to ensure that the practitioner does not overlook any of the required preprocessing techniques. Due to paper constraints, we cannot delve into the details of building each catalogue, hence a summary of the ML and preprocessing catalogues are presented in Table 1, and Table 2, respectively.

Table 1. Summary of the ML models catalogue.

	std	corr	skew	cat	missing	outliers
Linear/Logistic Regression	X	X	X	X	X	X
Lasso	X		X	X	X	
Ridge	X		X	X	X	X
Decision Tree						
Support Vector Machine	X		X	X	X	
Naive Bayes	X	X	X			X
K-Nearest neighbours	X			X	X	
Neural Network	X	X		X	X	X

Table 2. Summary of the preprocessing models catalogue.

	Diagnosis	Methods
Standardization	–	*StandardScaler, RobustScaler, MinMaxScaler, MaxAbsScaler*
Correlation	Pearson Coefficient [4]	Remove highly correlated variables
Skewness	K^2 statistic [8]	*BoxCox, YeoJohnson*
Categorical	–	*OneHotEncoder, OrdinalEncoder, TargetEncoding*
Missing Data	–	*SimpleImputer, KNNImputer, IterativeImputer*
Outliers	*LocalOutLierFactor*	Remove outliers

4   Conclusion

In this paper, we have presented a methodology which aims to guide the selection of the preprocessing techniques that are required or strongly recommended for the type of ML model chosen and the data at hand. Despite being in a preliminary state, we are convinced that this is the right direction to provide a more systematic approach to the preprocessing and development of ML solutions, hopefully contributing to the adoption of MLOps as the new standard approach to develop and deploy ML solutions as well as fostering the development of new data-centric approaches and tools. As such, we expect that once the catalogues are fully developed, the result will be not only an excellent resource for beginners, but a useful methodology for practitioners that greatly reduces the probability of overlooking required preprocessing techniques and saves valuable development time.

The next step is to reassure the value of the methodology in the real world. Hence, we will perform a user-study where data scientists, as well as students, use the methodology to develop an ML solution and provide feedback on it.

Even though the catalogues can already be of great value, as part of our future work we intend to research about sustainable ways to extend and maintain them. One possibility would be to create the catalogues in a collaborative fashion, distilling information about how ML models behave on different datasets and preprocessing combinations during the development of different ML systems. At the same time, we will extend the methodology into the field of Deep Learning (DL) [11], as DL models are gaining increasing popularity as they are giving excellent results for a variety of problems.

Acknowledgements. This work has been co-funded by the AETHER-UA project (PID2020-112540RB-C43), funded by Spanish Ministry of Science and Innovation, and the BALLADEER (PROMETEO/2021/088) project, funded by the Conselleria de Innovación, Universidades, Ciencia y Sociedad Digital (Generalitat Valenciana).

References

1. Data-Centric AI. https://datacentricai.org/. Accessed 10 Mar 2023
2. Alla, S., Adari, S.K.: What Is MLOps? In: Alla, S., Adari, S.K. (eds.) Beginning MLOps with MLFlow, pp. 79–124. Apress, Berkeley, CA (2021). https://doi.org/10.1007/978-1-4842-6549-9_3
3. Antonio, N., De Almeida, A., Nunes, L.: Predicting hotel booking cancellations to decrease uncertainty and increase revenue. Tour. Manag. Stud. **13**(2), 25–39 (2017)
4. Benesty, J., Chen, J., Huang, Y., Cohen, I.: Pearson correlation coefficient. In: Benesty, J., Chen, J., Huang, Y., Cohen, I. (eds.) Noise Reduction in Speech Processing, vol. 2, pp. 1–4. Springer, Heidelberg (2009). https://doi.org/10.1007/978-3-642-00296-0_5
5. Bishop, C.M., Nasrabadi, N.M.: Pattern Recognition and Machine Learning, vol. 4. Springer, New York (2006)
6. Box, G.E., Cox, D.R.: An analysis of transformations. J. Roy. Stat. Soc.: Ser. B (Methodol.) **26**(2), 211–243 (1964)
7. Crone, S.F., Lessmann, S., Stahlbock, R.: The impact of preprocessing on data mining: an evaluation of classifier sensitivity in direct marketing. Eur. J. Oper. Res. **173**(3), 781–800 (2006)
8. D'agostino, R.B., Belanger, A., D'Agostino, R.B., Jr.: A suggestion for using powerful and informative tests of normality. Am. Stat. **44**(4), 316–321 (1990)
9. Feurer, M., Eggensperger, K., Falkner, S., Lindauer, M., Hutter, F.: Auto-sklearn 2.0: the next generation. arXiv preprint arXiv:2007.04074 (2020)
10. Gonçalves, C.A., Gonçalves, C.T., Camacho, R., Oliveira, E.C.: The impact of pre-processing on the classification of MEDLINE documents. In: PRIS, pp. 53–61 (2010)
11. Goodfellow, I., Bengio, Y., Courville, A.: Deep Learning. MIT Press, Cambridge (2016). http://www.deeplearningbook.org
12. He, X., Zhao, K., Chu, X.: AutoML: a survey of the state-of-the-art. Knowl.-Based Syst. **212**, 106622 (2021)
13. James, G., Witten, D., Hastie, T., Tibshirani, R.: An Introduction to Statistical Learning, vol. 112. Springer, New York (2013). https://doi.org/10.1007/978-1-4614-7138-7
14. Kuhn, M., Johnson, K.: Feature Engineering and Selection: A Practical Approach for Predictive Models. CRC Press, Boca Raton (2019)

15. Kuhn, M., Johnson, K., et al.: Applied Predictive Modeling, vol. 26. Springer, New York (2013). https://doi.org/10.1007/978-1-4614-6849-3
16. Miao, Y.: Using machine learning algorithms to predict diabetes mellitus based on Pima Indians Diabetes dataset. In: 2021 the 5th International Conference on Virtual and Augmented Reality Simulations, pp. 47–53 (2021)
17. Pereira, P., Cunha, J., Fernandes, J.P.: On understanding data scientists. In: 2020 IEEE Symposium on Visual Languages and Human-Centric Computing (VL/HCC), pp. 1–5. IEEE (2020)
18. Uysal, A.K., Gunal, S.: The impact of preprocessing on text classification. Inf. Process. Manag. **50**(1), 104–112 (2014)
19. Wolpert, D.H., Macready, W.G.: No free lunch theorems for optimization. IEEE Trans. Evol. Comput. **1**(1), 67–82 (1997)
20. Yeo, I.K., Johnson, R.A.: A new family of power transformations to improve normality or symmetry. Biometrika **87**(4), 954–959 (2000)

Parsing Causal Models – An Instance Segmentation Approach

Jonas Scharfenberger[✉] and Burkhardt Funk

Institute of Information Systems, Leuphana University, Lüneburg, Germany
{jonas.scharfenberger,burkhardt.funk}@leuphana.de

Abstract. The steadily growing number of publications in the field of information systems as well as the confusion arising from the naming of theoretical concepts, complicate the process of literature reviewing. While several knowledge repositories and databases are developed to combat this issue, a considerable amount of manual effort to populate the databases is required. The information these tools seek to present is often compactly summarized in causal models with a graph-like structure (e.g., structural equation models). Our work aims to develop a graph parsing method that reduces the amount of manual effort required and thus builds a foundation towards an augmentation of knowledge extraction from causal models. We contribute to the ongoing efforts in developing graph parsing tools by proposing a novel instance segmentation-based approach that leverages a new method to generate annotated synthetic graph images. Our solution is evaluated on a dataset of 166 images of structural equation models and outperforms existing graph parsing approaches in this use case.

Keywords: Graph parsing · Instance segmentation · Structural equation models · Synthetic data

1 Introduction

In the literature review process, information systems scholars are typically confronted with two issues that complicate identifying relevant work: the "construct identity fallacy" [1] and the "jungle conundrum" [2]. The former describes the problem of different names referring to the identical theoretical construct or identical names referring to different theoretical constructs. The latter represents "the problem of identifying similar causal models from a growing knowledge repository" [2].

Advances addressing the construct identity problem propose databases and repositories (e.g., Inter-Nomological Network [1], DISKNET [3], and TheoryOn [4]) which seek to facilitate the exploration of similar constructs and construct relationships. The "jungle conundrum" is tackled by leveraging the underlying graph structure of causal models to measure their structural and semantic similarity [2]. However, all of these approaches require a substantial amount of human effort to extract the relevant information from the underlying articles.

C. Cabanillas and F. Perez (Eds.): CAiSE 2023, LNBIP 477, pp. 43–51, 2023.
https://doi.org/10.1007/978-3-031-34674-3_6

Thus, employing machine learning models to augment the knowledge extraction process has a high potential to reduce human effort and enlarge the amount of information readily available. Since the correctness of the information extracted is extremely important, rather than automating the knowledge extraction process, a human-in-the-loop solution is advisable.

In most cases, the investigated theoretical model is compactly summarized in a graphical representation of the model. These figures are potential data sources for tools to extract the required knowledge from the articles. Typically, these model figures have a graph-like structure, i.e., they consist of nodes containing textual information, directed edges, and optionally edge weights. Hence, such figures can be decomposed into n different 4-tuples (node$_1$, node$_2$, edge direction, edge weight), which graph parsing tools aim to reconstruct. Previous work seeking to augment the knowledge extraction task proposes tools that heavily rely on deep learning object detectors to recognize the graph structure [5,6]. Prominent approaches to parsing other graph-like figures [7,8] also build their solution on bounding box predictions. Most likely due to the substantial effort required to create segmentation annotations, deep learning segmentation approaches to these problems are not pursued yet.

We contribute to the ongoing efforts in tackling the "construct identity fallacy" and "jungle conundrum" by proposing a pipeline to parse figures of causal models. Thereby, we seek to ease the population of databases and repositories as well as the data gathering for further downstream tasks such as causal model similarity detection. We propose a novel technique[1] to generate synthetic datasets of graph images with segmentation labels and investigate the performance of deep learning segmentation models for parsing graphs.

2   Related Work

Various graph parsing solutions have been developed for different subclasses of graph-like figures [5–9]. Traditional computer vision approaches (e.g., [9]) to parse graph images rely on binarization and skeletonization techniques which typically have two downsides: stricter assumptions on the graph images have to be made and natural document noise (e.g., introduced by scanning figures contained in books) complicates the preprocessing steps. Thus, recent works train bounding box object detectors to recognize the graphs' structural elements and use rule-based algorithms to reconstruct the graph from the detected objects. Scharfenberger et al. [5] aim to extract knowledge from structural equation models (SEMs) by training a YOLOv4 model to detect path coefficients, latent and observed variables. However, since edges are not detected, they cannot reconstruct the graph structures. Schäfer et al. [7] develop a task-specific model architecture ("Arrow R-CNN") to transform handwritten diagrams into their digital counterparts. Arrow R-CNN is a Faster R-CNN [10] network extended by an additional head to predict the coordinates of the arrow keypoints (i.e., start and end points). Using the predicted keypoints and bounding boxes as well as the

---

[1] Code is available at https://github.com/purplesweatshirt/CMParsing.

text boxes extracted via an OCR engine, they use a distance-based heuristic to match nodes to edges and texts to detected objects. They evaluate their model based on the diagram recognition rate where a diagram is considered as recognized if a) the number of detected and ground truth symbols are equal, b) all symbols are correctly classified and match the ground truth position with an intersection over union threshold (IoU) of 80%, and c) each edge is matched to the correct nodes. In a related use-case, the Arrow R-CNN model is used to parse handwritten BPMN sketches [8]. They reconstruct 3-tuples (source node, target node, and edge) from the model's predictions and ignore the textual information in this work. Their solution is evaluated on a dataset of 92 hand-drawn BPMNs using the F_1 metric for shape and edge recognitions. Motivated by the challenges of training deep learning models on small datasets, Schölch et al. [6] suggest to generate synthetic datasets of graph-like figures. Their automatically labeled images are generated by randomly placing nodes, texts corresponding to nodes, edges between nodes, and corresponding edge weights on a canvas.

3 Proposed Solution

The knowledge repositories are manually populated mostly by graduate students and scientific staff who are provided simple input masks. Within the scope of our work, we develop a model that runs in the backend and enables pre-filling the input mask with predictions that can be corrected by the user[2]. Our model requires an image of the causal model and returns a graph representation. The fundamental design of our proposed solution (Fig. 1, red box) to parse figures of causal models is based on previous work [6–8] suggesting to tackle the problem in three steps: (1) detecting the elements of the graph , (2) extracting the text via an OCR engine, and (3) applying distance-based heuristics and further postprocessing steps to reconstruct the graph structure. Except for parts of the postprocessing, this solution could potentially be applied to other graph-like figures in future research. In the following, we present our technique to generate synthetic images (Sect. 3.1), our novel segmentation model as the core of the graph parsing tool (Sect. 3.2), and the postprocessing routine (Sect. 3.3).

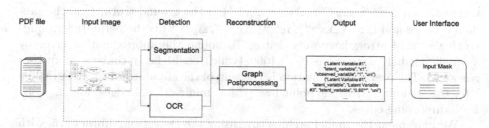

Fig. 1. The proposed workflow. The scope of our work is located in the red box. (Color figure online)

---

[2] A demo of such an augmented input mask will be presented at the conference.

3.1   Synthetic Dataset

To enhance previous work [6], we seek to generate more realistic images of graph-like figures by (1) utilizing graph rendering engines rather than randomly placing objects, (2) augmenting the images with "document noise", and (3) annotating the images automatically with segmentation masks.

We randomly choose a number of nodes, node names from a list of English words, and a random set of node pairs that shall be connected via an edge. The GraphViz rendering algorithm determines the position of nodes and edges in the image. We randomly alter various graph rendering attributes (see our implementation for more details) to create a diverse set of images. We use the meta-data (i.e., node position, connected edges, various shape attributes, and texts) produced by the GraphViz engine to automatically reconstruct segmentation masks of nodes and edges and thereby extend the previous synthetic data generation approach. Since real figures may originate from scanned document pages, we extend the synthetic dataset by augmenting a random subset of 25% of the images with "natural document noise". We collect images of document backgrounds from two public Kaggle datasets [13,14] and replace each white pixel in the generated graph figure with the noisy document backgrounds and apply Gaussian blurring to the images.

3.2   Arrow Mask R-CNN Model

We propose the *Arrow Mask R-CNN* model architecture (Fig. 2), which extends the Arrow R-CNN architecture [7] by an additional segmentation head. Since the original loss of Arrow R-CNN is not explicitly designed for bidirectional edges, we adjust the loss function and make the architecture applicable to a broader range of graphs. We use a differentiable approximation of the minimum to account for bidirectional edges:

$$\mathcal{L}_{arw-bi} := \frac{1}{4N} \sum_{i=1}^{N} \frac{-1}{k} \log \left(e^{-k \cdot \sum_{d=1}^{4} (t_i[d] - \hat{t}_i[d])^2} + e^{-k \cdot \sum_{d=1}^{4} (\tilde{t}_i[d] - \hat{t}_i[d])^2} \right), \quad (1)$$

where $t_i := \left(\Delta x^{head}, \Delta y^{head}, \Delta x^{tail}, \Delta y^{tail} \right)$ is the ground-truth, $\hat{t}_i$ is the predicted vector and $\tilde{t}_i := \left(\Delta x^{tail}, \Delta y^{tail}, \Delta x^{head}, \Delta y^{head} \right)$ is the permuted ground-truth vector of arrow keypoints deltas. To bound the approximation error by a small number, we choose $k = 1000$ (which could be optimized in further research). The overall loss function is the sum of the standard Mask R-CNN loss [16], the standard arrow keypoint loss [7] for unidirectional edges, and $\mathcal{L}_{arw-bi}$ for bidirectional edges.

We implement the model architecture using the Detectron2 library [15] with the default ResNet-50-FPN backbone. Our training dataset consists of approx. 10k synthetic images and contains four different classes (uni- and bidirectional edges, edge weights, and nodes). The images are augmented by adding document noise, gaussian blurring (see Sect. 3.1), and horizontal flipping. We train the

Arrow Mask R-CNN model for 100k iterations using an SGD optimizer with a learning rate of 0.0025, a momentum of 0.9, and a weight decay of 0.0005.

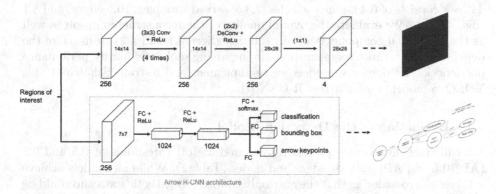

Fig. 2. Our Arrow Mask R-CNN architecture with exemplary outputs. The Arrow R-CNN branch (adopted from [7]) predicts class labels and deltas for boxes and keypoints.

3.3   Matching, Text Extraction and Node Classification

The model's outputs (class, confidence, bounding box, segmentation mask, arrow keypoints) must be further processed and supplemented by text detections to reconstruct the desired 4-tuples. First, we loop over all detected edges and nodes and calculate the pairwise distances. The two nodes having the minimal distance to the start and end keypoint are matched to the corresponding edge. Similarly, for every edge, we calculate the distances between the boundary points of the edge segmentation mask and the center points of all edge weight bounding boxes and match the closest edge weight to the edge. Second, we apply the PaddleOCR [17] engine to extract texts from the graph images. A text is matched to nodes or edges if the text lies within the object's bounding box or if the text and object have an IoU of more than 0.5. Furthermore, we concatenate the detected edge weights with unmatched texts that are purely numerical to minimize a loss of information. Third, the detected nodes are classified (latent or observed variable) using a Support Vector Machine (SVM). We extract the following features from the detected texts and objects: relative position in the image, relative area of the node, number of total characters, upper-case letters, words, and digits. The SVM is trained with a radial basis function kernel on a dataset of 4320 node names. The 4-tuples are then constructed from the matched objects and texts.

4   Evaluation

We base the evaluation of our graph parsing solution on images of SEMs since there are entire knowledge repositories dedicated to SEM-related research (e.g.,

DISKNET) and due to their importance in IS research [11]. We use a dataset of 166 published SEM figures from DISKNET [3], which are manually annotated following the 4-tuple logic explained above. On average, an SEM figure in our dataset consists of 6.4 latent variables, 2.3 observed variables, 10.5 edges, and 8.1 edge weights. We evaluate the overall quality of the reconstructed graph as well as the individual components of our solution (Sect. 4.1 and 4.2) to measure the benefits of an instance segmentation graph parsing tool and identify perfomance bottlenecks. As reference models we re-implement and re-train Schölch et al.'s YOLOv5 model [6] and Arrow R-CNN [7].

4.1   Evaluation of the Detection Model

We calculate the average precision measured at IoU thresholds of 0.5 and 0.8 (AP@0.5 and AP@0.8) for edges and nodes (Table 1). While all models achieve solid results considering that they are only trained on synthetic data and could be further fine-tuned on manually annotated images, our model achieves the highest AP scores. All three approaches show considerable drops in edge detection when the IoU threshold is increased. However, recognized edges with lower IoU scores may still be matched to the correct nodes.

4.2   Evaluation of the Matching

A 3-tuple ($node_1$, $node_2$, edge direction) is considered to be correct if (1) for both nodes the IoU of the predicted bounding box and ground truth bounding box exceeds 0.8, and (2) the predicted and ground truth edge direction are equal. Similarly, a 4-tuple ($node_1$, $node_2$, edge weight, edge direction) is considered correct if the aforementioned conditions are satisfied and if (3) the IoU of the ground truth and predicted edge weight bounding box is greater than 0.5 or if the predicted and ground truth texts match. The alternative condition is included due to the small size of edge weights.

The considerably lower precision and recall scores (Table 2) show that the matching algorithm introduces many errors. Our approach outperforms the reference models in reconstructing 3-tuples and 4-tuples and achieves comparably solid results (recall of 0.675 resp. 0.46). We argue that the poor performance of the reference models is due to the information used to calculate distances between nodes, edges, and weights. Overlapping and large bounding boxes of edges can cause unreliable distance measures and false matches. The performance of our model suggests that using segmentation masks as a basis to match edges, weights, and nodes can enhance the graph reconstruction performance.

4.3   Evaluation of the Graph Reconstruction

We evaluate the overall graph reconstruction by defining the following three conditions to consider a 4-tuple correct: (1) the extracted texts of nodes and edge weights match the ground truth text annotation, (2) the node class is predicted correctly, and (3) the predicted edge direction is correct.

Table 1. Average precision of the node and edge class measured at two IoU thresholds.

Approach	Node AP@0.5	Edge AP@0.5	Node AP@0.8	Edge AP@0.8
Schölch et al. [6]	0.851	0.503	0.818	0.245
Schäfer et al. [7]	0.878	0.694	0.829	0.243
Ours	**0.887**	**0.697**	**0.853**	**0.254**

Table 2. Mean recall and precision of the 3-tuple and 4-tuple reconstruction step.

Approach	Recall (3-tuple)	Prec. (3-tuple)	Recall (4-tuple)	Prec. (4-tuple)
Schölch et al. [6]	0.612	0.533	0.231	0.23
Schäfer et al. [7]	0.625	0.372	0.2	0.124
Ours	**0.675**	**0.599**	**0.46**	**0.344**

Incorporating the extracted texts from the OCR engine further decreases recall and precision (0.144 resp. 0.118) and can be seen as the bottleneck of our approach's solution. Nonetheless, our approach has the potential to reduce the required human labor, as demonstrated in the following two cases. First, by letting the human supervisor extract and match edge weights, our predictions achieve a recall of 0.378 and a precision of 0.312. Second, if we relax the first condition and consider texts having a total editing distance (Levenshtein distance [18]) of less than 6 correct, our approach scores a recall of 0.436 and a precision of 0.346. While both scenarios slightly increase the amount of human intervention, the total human effort could still be decreased relative to the status quo.

5   Conclusion and Future Work

Our work builds a foundation towards a *human-in-the-loop approach* to populate knowledge databases (e.g., DISKNET, INN, and TheoryOn) and gather the required data for downstream machine learning models (e.g., [2]). We present a novel solution to analyze graphical representations of SEMs and contribute to ongoing efforts to develop solutions for graph parsing in a twofold manner: (1) we improve existing approaches for *synthetic graph image generation*, and (2) we introduce the *Arrow Mask R-CNN* - a segmentation extension of [7] which is also capable of handling bidirectional edges.

Our proposed graph parsing pipeline is thoroughly evaluated on a dataset of 166 images of SEMs. While existing approaches, on average, correctly reconstruct 20–23.1% of a graph's 4-tuples (excluding the text), our approach correctly reconstructs 46% of the 4-tuples. Thus, we deduce that the more granular information provided by the segmentation masks is beneficial in the erroneous matching of the detected objects. However, the overall reconstruction results show that an automation of knowledge extraction from figures of causal models is currently not feasible. We strongly promote a human-in-the-loop approach, which employs our model to generate proposals that can be confirmed, modified, or supplemented by human intervention. Such a cyber-human system can modernize the hitherto time-consuming and tedious manual workflow of information retrieval from causal models while maintaining high quality extractions.

Two areas for future research emerge from our work. First, we will implement a user input mask supporting our tool and evaluate the entire workflow by conducting a field study to measure the time saved. Second, to mitigate the accumulation of errors across the post-processing steps, a fully-trainable model architecture that outputs a set of 4-tuples may be investigated.

References

1. Larsen, K., Bong, C.H.: A tool for addressing construct identity in literature reviews and meta-analyses. MIS Q. **40**, 529–551 (2016)
2. Song, Y., Watson, R.T., Zhao, X.: Literature reviewing: addressing the jingle and jangle fallacies and jungle conundrum using graph theory and NLP. In: ICIS 2021 Proceedings (2021)
3. Dann, D., et al.: DISKNET - a platform for the systematic accumulation of knowledge in IS research. In: ICIS 2019 Proceedings (2019)
4. Li, J., Larsen, K., Abbasi, A.: TheoryOn: a design framework and system for unlocking behavioral knowledge through ontology learning. MIS Q. **44**(4), 1733–1772 (2020)
5. Scharfenberger, J., Funk, B., Mueller, B.: The augmented theorist - toward automated knowledge extraction from conceptual models. In: ICIS 2021 Proceedings (2021)
6. Schölch, L., et al.: Towards automatic parsing of structured visual content through the use of synthetic data (2022). arXiv:2204.14136
7. Schäfer, B., Keuper, M., Stuckenschmidt, H.: Arrow R-CNN for handwritten diagram recognition. IJDAR **24**, 3–17 (2021)
8. Schäfer, B., van der Aa, H., Leopold, H., Stuckenschmidt, H.: Sketch2BPMN: automatic recognition of hand-drawn BPMN models. In: La Rosa, M., Sadiq, S., Teniente, E. (eds.) CAiSE 2021. LNCS, vol. 12751, pp. 344–360. Springer, Cham (2021). https://doi.org/10.1007/978-3-030-79382-1_21
9. Auer, C., Bachmaier, C., Brandenburg, F.J., Gleißner, A., Reislhuber, J.: Optical graph recognition. In: Didimo, W., Patrignani, M. (eds.) GD 2012. LNCS, vol. 7704, pp. 529–540. Springer, Heidelberg (2013). https://doi.org/10.1007/978-3-642-36763-2_47
10. Ren, S., He, K., Girshick, R., Sun, J.: Faster R-CNN: towards real-time object detection with region proposal networks. In Proceedings of NIPS2015, pp. 91–99 (2015)
11. Urbach, N., Ahlemann, F.: Structural equation modeling in information systems research using partial least squares. JITTA **11**(2), 5–40 (2010)
12. Graphviz Homepage. https://graphviz.org/. Accessed 16 Nov 2022
13. The largest historical handwritten digit dataset with 250k digits. https://www.kaggle.com/datasets/ayavariabdi/didadataset. Accessed 16 Nov 2022
14. Real World Documents Collections. https://www.kaggle.com/datasets/shaz13/real-world-documents-collections. Accessed 16 Nov 2022
15. Wu, Y., et al.: Detectron2. https://github.com/facebookresearch/detectron2. Accessed 16 Nov 2022

16. He, K., Gkioxari, G., Dollár, P., Girshick, R.: Mask R-CNN. In: IEEE International Conference on Computer Vision (ICCV) 2017, pp. 2980–2988 (2017)
17. Du, Y., et al.: PP-OCRv2: bag of tricks for ultra lightweight OCR system (2021). arxiv:2109.03144
18. Levenshtein, V.I.: Binary codes capable of correcting deletions, insertions and reversals. In: Soviet Physics Doklady, vol. 10, no. 8, pp. 707–710 (1966)

Visualising Personal Data Flows: Insights from a Case Study of Booking.com

Haiyue Yuan[1]([✉])(ID), Matthew Boakes[1](ID), Xiao Ma[2], Dongmei Cao[2](ID), and Shujun Li[1](ID)

[1] Institute of Cyber Security for Society (iCSS) & School of Computing, University of Kent, Canterbury, UK
{h.yuan-211,m.j.boakes,s.j.li}@kent.ac.uk
[2] Nottingham Business School, Nottingham Trent University, Nottingham, UK
{xiao.ma,dongmei.cao}@ntu.ac.uk

Abstract. Commercial organisations are holding and processing an ever-increasing amount of personal data. Policies and laws are continually changing to require these companies to be more transparent regarding collection, storage, processing and sharing of this data. This paper reports our work of taking Booking.com as a case study to visualise personal data flows extracted from their privacy policy. By showcasing how the company shares its consumers' personal data, we raise questions and extend discussions on the challenges and limitations of using privacy policies to inform online users about the true scale and the landscape of personal data flows. This case study can inform us about future research on more data flow-oriented privacy policy analysis and on the construction of a more comprehensive ontology on personal data flows in complicated business ecosystems.

Keywords: Personal data · Data flow · Privacy policy · Privacy · Data sharing · Travel

1 Introduction

Despite the existence of information security policies and data protection laws such as the EU's GDPR (General Data Protection Regulation), over-collection and breach of personal data are constantly happening in the online world. Such data privacy and security issues are partly due to the complex nature of data collection, processing and sharing processes, where multiple parties are involved and the data owner (more formally called "data subjects") often has no clear view of how their personal data flow between different entities. When the consumer uses a social media (e.g., Facebook) account to register for an online service, there will

Supported by the EPSRC (Engineering and Physical Sciences Research Council, part of the UKRI) under the grant numbers EP/R033749/1 and EP/R033609/1. The full edition of this paper can be found on arXiv.org as a preprint at: https://arxiv.org/abs/2304.09603.

be further personal data shared between the social media company (e.g., Meta) and the service provider. However, the biggest data privacy and security threat caused by the complex situation of personal data sharing among multiple parties [14] is not sufficiently studied in the literature. A recent study [7] investigated such complexity in the tourism domain, and suggested that, while collecting and using personal data can result in more appealing tourism offers and more efficient travel, it can also lead to security risks and privacy concerns, thereby discouraging some travellers from sharing their personal data with service providers. To that end, it will help if travellers are made aware of what personal data will be collected and shared with whom for what purposes. A common approach is to present a privacy policy to users, and some past studies looked into privacy policies in different perspectives such as their impact on users' privacy perception, attitude and behaviour [2,6], automate privacy policy analysis [1,3,5], and readability and visualisation [1,3,10]. However, the current approaches are fragmented without comprehensively addressing the full scale of the personal data collection and sharing flows. Having this in mind, the main research question of this paper is: *Can we extract and visualise personal data flows from and to multiple parties involved from the analysis of a privacy policy?*

To answer this research question, we used Booking.com as an example to obtain in-depth insights with the visual- aid to understand how a user's personal data can be collected by Booking.com and other associated organisations. We present the following contributions: 1) we propose an approach to systematically analysing and reconstructing personal data flows declared in a privacy policy; 2) we report insights of personal data flows among multiple parties via a simple data visualisation approach to better inform online users about the landscape and key points of a privacy policy; 3) we highlight the needs to have a more in-depth investigation of privacy policies from other relevant organisations to get a more comprehensive understanding of personal data flows; and 4) we report lessons learnt from this case study and future research directions.

2   Related Work

The law in many countries, such as the GDPR in EU member states and the UK, requires services to provide privacy policies when collecting personal data is involved, and such privacy policies should be presented in a concise, transparent, intelligible, and easily accessible form. Researchers have been investigated privacy policies in relation to consumers from various perspectives such as its impact on privacy concerns and attitudes, and its visualisation and readability. Bracamonte et al. [2] experimentally evaluated the effects of explanatory information on the perception of the results of an automated privacy policy tool. The results indicate that justification information increases behavioural intention and perceptions of credibility and utility. Kitkowska et al. [9] studied the influence of privacy policy's visual design by conducting an online experiment and revealed that people feel powerless when acknowledging notices and have no choice but to agree. Ibdah et al. [6] studied the users' attitudes and opinions regarding privacy rules. The results suggested that the primary motivation for users to read the privacy policy are the concerns about the service providers. To improve the readability of privacy policy, Reinhardt et al. [10] developed interactive privacy policies based on the concept of nutrition labels. Harkous et al. [5] proposed an automated framework for privacy policy analysis (Polisis) based on deep learning. Similarly, Andow et al. [1] developed PolicyLint, a framework that can automatically generate ontologies from privacy policies through the use of sentence-level natural language processing.

Furthermore, there is also research work investigating how to best store and manage the personal data. For instance, Verbrugge et al. [11] examined the possibility for a "personal data vault society" and the steps necessary to realise this vision. Fallatah et al. [4] reviewed existing work on personal data stores (PDS), which allow individuals to store, control, and manage their data. They argued that one of the technical barriers is the data flow management among different parties. In addition, another way to consolidate the understanding of privacy and personal data collection/sharing is to develop graphical models. More recently, a graphical model developed by Lu et al. [13] can evaluate personal data flows from "me" (a specific user) and values flowing back to "me" to help inform "me" about the privacy-benefit trade-offs.

3   Methodology

In this work, we proposed constructing possible flows of personal data through the analysis of an online service provider's privacy policy. By visually representing a personal data flow graph derived from the privacy policy, we intend to reveal some potentially overlooked details of personal data sharing activities of consumers of the online service. We decided to use the privacy policy of Booking.com[1] as a case study based on the following reasons: 1) Booking.com has the highest revenue globally within the online travel market and is the largest online travel agency by booking volume[2]; 2) Booking.com provides a range of features and has a close link with many other subsidiaries of its parent company, Booking Holding Inc., therefore being a good case for understanding how personal data are shared between multiple parties. 3) Booking.com deals with its customers' personal data regularly due to the nature of its business model. This requires its privacy policy to provide more details on how their consumers' personal data are collected, processed and shared.

To better facilitate the personal data flow mapping and visualisation, we adopted a simplified version of the graphical model proposed in [13] with the main aim of establishing the relationships between the following entities of different types: a) *Person* entities stand for natural people in the physical world; b) *Data* entities stand to atomic data items about one or more person entities; c) *Service* entities refer to different physical and online services that serve people

---

[1] https://www.booking.com/content/privacy.en-gb.html
[2] https://www.researchandmarkets.com/reports/5330849/global-online-travel-market-2022

for a specific purpose; d) *Organisation* entities refer to organisations that relate to one or more services. We analysed the privacy policy from the perspective of how personal data flows from users of Booking.com to different data-consuming entities including Booking.com and other organisation entities. More specifically, we analysed the privacy policy from the following two main perspectives: 1) **data collection** is about how Booking.com can implicitly and explicitly collect personal data from its users, and how Booking.com may also receive indirect data about its customers from other sources. 2) **data sharing** is about how Booking.com share personal data collected with third parties, including within Booking Holdings Inc. and its other subsidiaries, and with other third parties and social media service providers. By manually noting down the relationships between different entities while going through the whole privacy policy, we were able to derive a graphical representation of possible personal data flows and a visualisation of the graph. It is worth noting that the graph presented in this paper is a simplified version, which is based on the assumption that the booker, referring to an individual who arranges a travel booking, is also the sole traveller. It is important to acknowledge that the personal data flows and the data flow graph can be more complicated when the booker is not a traveller or a member of a large group of travellers.

4   Results

Figure 1 shows the reconstructed personal data flows through the decoding of the privacy policy of Booking.com in terms of personal data sharing within the context of travellers (users of the service). As indicated by the green arrows at top of the figure, the personal data flows from the left to the right side of the figure, demonstrating how Booking.com can collect its customers' personal data, what types of personal data can be collected by Booking.com, and to what extent Booking.com shares customers' personal data with external parties for what purposes. In addition, we also used 'C1', 'C2' and 'C3' in the diagram to represent the three main challenges that we have identified in different aspects of personal data flows through the analysis of the privacy policy.

4.1   How Personal Data Is Collected by Booking.com

As illustrated in Fig. 1, Booking.com can collect customers' personal data from various sources in several ways. We categorise them into two groups based on the original data controller (the service provider who collected customer data in the first place): *direct data collection* and *indirect data collection*. It is worth noting that all data types listed in *Data Boxes A, B, C, D* of the figure are extracted from examples in the privacy policy. However, we acknowledge that it is not an exhaustive list of the data types Booking.com may collect. We added three dots at the bottom of Data Box D to indicate such incompleteness and also considered this as one of the challenges (i.e., C1 in Fig. 1), deserving further studies. We provide more details throughout the rest of this section.

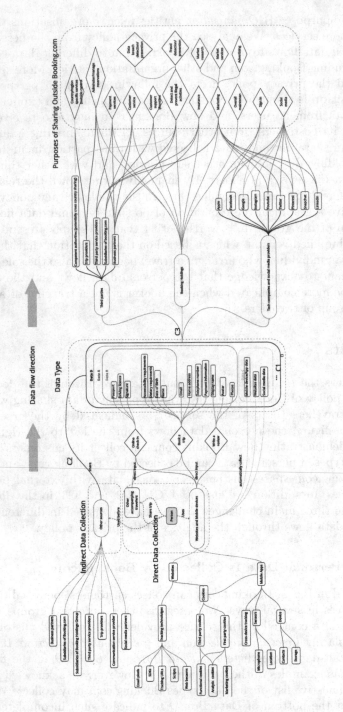

Fig. 1. Booking.com personal data flows diagram extracted from its privacy policy

1) *Direct data collection* refers to the observation that Booking.com collects a person's information/data directly from a source. We further identified two approaches of direct data collection. a) *Explicit direct data collection* means that a person or other traveller provides data to Booking.com directly via its website or mobile app as illustrated in Fig. 1. Data Box A contains personal data that could be collected specifically for the booking purposes such as the booker's names, telephone number, and email address. Data Box B includes information of the traveller such as their name, date of birth, email address, and dietary requirements. b) *Implicit direct data collection* means that, without explicitly data input from a person, Booking.com automatically collects data, which is occurring simultaneously while a person is using Booking.com's website or mobile app. As depicted in *Data Box C* in Fig. 1, such data could include behavioural data of the user when using a mobile device, the website or the mobile app, the user's social media data, IP addresses, and language settings on the devices, which can be automatically collected using different technologies such as web tracking technologies, cookies, device sensors and cross-device tracking technologies.

2) *Indirect data collection* refers to personal data that is not directly collected by Booking.com due to a booker's use of its website or mobile app, but shared with Booking.com by other parties such as third-party service providers, associated business partners, and other subsidiaries of Booking Holdings Inc. Please note that these parties' privacy policies could have explicitly allowed sharing of their consumers' personal data with Booking.com. Thereby, the user's various data as demonstrated in Data Box D block in Fig. 1 could be shared with Booking.com and be used together with the data directly collected by Booking.com in order to provide enhanced customer experience and better services. Here, we would like to highlight that Data Box D may contain a much more comprehensive range of personal data, since Booking.com can still gain access to many personal data of their customers indirectly from other third parties. As stated in Booking.com's privacy policy, it is worth noting that how and what other third-party organisations share personal data with Booking.com depends on their business needs and privacy policies. In other words, it is impossible to get more insights about such personal data without analysing privacy policies from other third-party organisations, which is needed to recover the full scale of indirect data collection. We consider this as another challenge (i.e., C2 in Fig. 1) for future research.

4.2   How Booking.com Share Data with Other Parties

Booking.com claims to collaborate with various parties to provide smooth and satisfactory customer service and serve other cooperative purposes. One crucial way to facilitate this is to share customer data with external parties. By analysing the privacy policy of Booking.com, we have identified three main destinations for data sharing: third-party associates, the Booking Holdings group and its subsidiaries, and tech companies and social media providers.

1) Third party associates: There are different types of third parties according to Booking.com's privacy policy, and each type has its specific purpose of utilising the personal data shared by Booking.com to fulfil users' booking activities. For instance, the personal data can be shared with central/local authorities for legal requirements or legislation compliance; and Booking.com outsources its administration/reservation services and customer services to a business partner, which would require sharing of some personal data to facilitate such outsourced services.

2) Booking Holdings and its subsidiaries: Being a subsidiary of Booking Holdings Inc., Booking.com can share its users' personal data upward to its parent company. Booking Holdings Inc. provides travel-related services to people in more than 220 countries and territories through many subsidiaries such as Priceline, Agoda, Rentalcars.com, and Momondo[3]. These subsidiaries of Booking Holdings Inc. offer some essential services to each other, and personal data collected by Booking.com may be further spread to other subsidiaries in order to provide more sophisticated combinations of services, as shown in Fig. 1, including payment services, admin/manage reservations, customer service, customer support, illegal activity detection and prevention.

3) Technology companies and social media providers: Personal data can be shared with technology companies and social media service providers in exchange for their services or to provide extra customer benefits. For example, Booking.com allows its customers to sign in using their Apple, Facebook, or Google credentials. In addition, using social media features such as integrating social media plugins into the Booking.com website/mobile app and social media messaging services can lead to the exchange of personal data between Booking.com and the social media service providers (e.g., Instagram, YouTube, and Twitter). Moreover, another important purpose of such personal data sharing is to conduct market research and provide more personalised market and advertising services.

However, the privacy policy does not contain any information about which type of personal data are shared with which other organisations in details preventing us from achieving a full understanding of the landscape of personal data collection and sharing. Thereby, we envisage that another challenge (i.e., C3 in Fig. 1) for future work is to conduct more work to study cross-organisational data sharing to consolidate our understanding.

5   Further Discussions and Conclusion

The paper presents a case study to understand understand how Booking.com collects and shares personal data based on analysis of its privacy policy. By producing a personal data flow graph as a visual aid, we were able to reveal how Booking.com can collect personal data and share such data with other organisations. Although our work focuses on Booking.com as a case study, the following lessons learned are likely true for many other online services regarding

---

[3] https://www.bookingholdings.com/about/factsheet/

the challenges of refining privacy policies to reflect the landscape of personal data collection and sharing: 1) the lack of a comprehensive description of the types of personal data that could be collected directly or indirectly; 2) an incomplete description of how and to what extent other organisations can share personal data with online service providers; 3) an unclear description of how and to what extend online services can share their customers' personal data with other third parties; 4) an unclear disclosure on how personal data collected are used. The lack of clarity and transparency makes it difficult for users to understand the full extent of personal data sharing and how their personal data may be used, therefore subsequently harming their confidence in continuously accepting this business-centric approach to personal data management of online services' users.

Furthermore, this study has the following limitations, and we intend to address these in our future work: 1) we only considered using the privacy policy as the main data source to derive the data, which is not enough in reality; 2) some fine-grained details of personal data flows were not presented to avoid over-complicating the diagram; and 3) a user study should be conducted to validate our approach. Last but not the least, we intend consider this work as the basis to establish a general approach to automating extraction of personal data flow generation for online services. We hope that this case study can be a stepping stone to elicit more follow-up work on privacy policy analysis, personal data flows, and related graphical modelling and ontological research.

References

1. Andow, B., et al.: PolicyLint: investigating internal privacy policy contradictions on Google Play. In: Proceedings of USENIX Security 2019, pp. 585–602 (2019). https://www.usenix.org/conference/usenixsecurity19/presentation/andow
2. Bracamonte, V., Hidano, S., Tesfay, W.B., Kiyomoto, S.: Effects of explanatory information on privacy policy summarization tool perception. In: Furnell, S., Mori, P., Weippl, E., Camp, O. (eds.) ICISSP 2020. CCIS, vol. 1545, pp. 156–177. Springer, Cham (2022). https://doi.org/10.1007/978-3-030-94900-6_8
3. Carlsson, R., et al.: Where does your data go? comparing network traffic and privacy policies of public sector mobile applications. In: Proceedings of WorldCIST 2022, vol. 1. pp. 214–225. Springer, Cham (2022). https://doi.org/10.1007/978-3-031-04826-5_21
4. Fallatah, K.U., et al.: Personal data stores (PDS): a review. Sensors 23(3) (2023). https://doi.org/10.3390/s23031477
5. Harkous, H., et al.: Polisis: automated analysis and presentation of privacy policies using deep learning. In: Proceedings of USENIX Security 2018, pp. 531–548 (2018). https://www.usenix.org/conference/usenixsecurity18/presentation/harkous
6. Ibdah, D., et al.: Why should I read the privacy policy, I just need the service: a study on attitudes and perceptions toward privacy policies. IEEE Access 9, 166465–166487 (2021). https://doi.org/10.1109/ACCESS.2021.3130086
7. Ioannou, A., et al.: That's private! understanding travelers' privacy concerns and online data disclosure. J. Travel Res. 60(7), 1510–1526 (2021). https://doi.org/10.1177/0047287520951642

8. Jin, H., et al.: Why are they collecting my data? Inferring the purposes of network traffic in mobile apps. In: Proceedings of the ACM on Interactive, Mobile, Wearable and Ubiquitous Technologies, vol. 2, no. 4 (2018). https://doi.org/10.1145/3287051
9. Kitkowska, A., et al.: Enhancing privacy through the visual design of privacy notices: Exploring the interplay of curiosity, control and affect. In: Proceedings of SOUPS 2020. USENIX Association (2020). https://www.usenix.org/conference/soups2020/presentation/kitkowska
10. Reinhardt, D., et al.: Visual interactive privacy policy: the better choice? In: Proceedings of CHI 2021, ACM (2021). https://doi.org/10.1145/3411764.3445465
11. Verbrugge, S., et al.: Towards a personal data vault society: an interplay between technological and business perspectives. In: Proceedings of FITCE 2021, IEEE (2021). https://doi.org/10.1109/FITCE53297.2021.9588540
12. Wieringa, J., et al.: Data analytics in a privacy-concerned world. J. Bus. Res. **122**, 915–925 (2021). https://doi.org/10.1016/j.jbusres.2019.05.005
13. Lu, Y., Li, S.: From data flows to privacy-benefit trade-offs: a user-centric semantic model. Secur. Priv. **5**(4) (2022). https://doi.org/10.1002/spy2.225
14. Such, J.M., Criado, N.: Resolving multi-party privacy conflicts in social media. IEEE Trans. Knowl. Data Eng. **28**(7), 1851–1863 (2016). https://doi.org/10.1109/TKDE.2016.2539165

Rsourcer: Scaling Feedback on Research Drafts

Yuchao Jiang[1]([✉]), Boualem Benatallah[1,2], and Marcos Báez[3]

[1] University of New South Wales, Sydney, Australia
yuchao.jiang@unsw.edu.au
[2] Dublin City University, Dublin, Ireland
boualem.benatallah@dcu.ie
[3] Bielefeld University of Applied Sciences, Bielefeld, Germany
marcos.baez@fh-bielefeld.de

Abstract. Effective feedback is crucial for early-stage researchers (ESRs) to develop their research skills. While feedback from supervisors and colleagues is important, additional feedback from external helpers can be beneficial. However, obtaining diverse and high-quality feedback outside of a research group can be challenging. In this work, we designed and prototyped Rsourcer, a crowdsourcing-based pipeline that simplifies the process of requesting, offering, evaluating, and adopting feedback. We evaluated Rsourcer with a concept validation study and a pilot study, which showed its potential. This work contributes with insights into crowdsourcing support with social technologies and extends research on scaling support for skills development.

Keywords: Sociotechnical systems · feedback · crowdsourcing

1 Introduction

Feedback on research drafts is important for developing research skills, especially for early-stage researchers (ESRs), who are typically PhD students [15]. However, dedicated on-demand feedback from advisors is hardly scalable since advisors have limited time and resources [18]. External feedback from beyond a research group is often desired and perceived to help learn from diverse viewpoints [9].

Literature has explored scaling the feedback. For example, some research initiatives [14,18] and platforms (e.g., ResearchGate Q&A site[1]) have explored leveraging crowdsourcing techniques to scale research feedback by affording help from beyond supervisory teams. However, voluntarily contributing good-quality feedback on research papers takes time, effort and knowledge about how to offer good-quality feedback [6,8].

We aim to crowdsource feedback at scale without increasing the helpers' burden and assuring feedback quality. We address these gaps by distributing the

---

[1] https://www.researchgate.net/.

C. Cabanillas and F. Perez (Eds.): CAiSE 2023, LNBIP 477, pp. 61–68, 2023.
https://doi.org/10.1007/978-3-031-34674-3_8

feedback in online communities and affording the helpers to support the ESRs collaboratively. More especifically, informed by our preliminary studies [8,9] and literature, we introduce Rsourcer, a system that scales feedback with crowdsourcing, streamlining the process of requesting, providing and interpreting feedback. Furthermore, we designed a prototype that instantiates the proposed crowdsourcing pipeline with user interfaces. We evaluated Rsourcer with a concept validation study and a pilot study. The primary contributions of this paper include:

- A crowdsourcing pipeline that scales feedback on research papers and streamlines the process of requesting, providing and interpreting feedback.
- A prototype that instantiates the pipeline and demonstrates the application of crowdsourcing in feedback exchange for research artefacts.
- Evaluations, including a concept validation study and a pilot study, showing the promise of Rsourcer and revealing insights for future research on feedback exchange on research papers.

2   Rsourcer Pipeline and Prototype Design

2.1   Design Challenges

To gain insight into the research skill development practices and challenges of ESRs, we first conducted in-depth semi-structured interviews with 27 ESRs from various academic disciplines [8]. Building upon the interview findings, we conducted an online survey with 120 ESRs of diverse backgrounds [9]. We summarised the results from these studies [8,9] in Table 1, as primary design challenges (C#) that led to the general requirements (R#):

Table 1. The challenges matrix designed for the survey

Requesting Feedback	C1	Suspicion of online helpers' intentions to give feedback
	C2	Fear of appearing incompetent with a public profile
	C3	Disappointment and frustration when not receiving responses
	C4	Fear of confidentiality/IP issues when sharing research online.
Engaging in discussions	C5	Slow response time while discussing research artifacts, leading to unproductive and unfruitful feedback conversations
	C6	Limitations in properly explaining inquiries and understanding helpers' feedback in text-based interactions.
Adopting Feedback	C7	Ambiguity of the helpers' qualification to answer inquiries
	C8	Feedback quality not up to scientific standards
	C9	Online help failing to provide precise and complete answers
	C10	Feedback not timely for deadlines

R1 **Guide ESRs in elaborating feedback requests** to optimize the effort required to create effective and clear requests (C6, C7). This will increase the chances of receiving the necessary feedback (C3) while reducing the need for further clarification (C5).

R2 **Build on trusted networks and communities** to address issues of suspicion and trust (C1, C4) while creating a secure space for ESRs to request feedback (C3). ESRs should have control over the assignment process, as well as the visibility of their requests and profiles (C2, C7).

R3 **Support helpers in providing high-quality, timely feedback** by enabling them to work on smaller review assignments, complement and collaborate on each other's reviews (C5, C9, C10). Feedback reporting should also be guided, ensuring that the feedback aligns with ESRs' feedback needs.

R4 **Assist ESRs in interpreting and reflecting on feedback** by integrating a feedback evaluation process that helps them identify high-quality and appropriate feedback from reliable sources (C7, C8, C9).

2.2 Crowsourcing-based Pipeline

Informed by the preliminary studies, resulting requirements (R1-R4) and literature (e.g., [10,18]), we developed a crowdsourcing-based process and tool to support ESRs feedback elicitation needs (see Fig. 1). Rsourcer builds on socio-technical services [7] to afford scaling support for ESRs to develop their research skills. It supports research communities to exchange feedback on their research drafts online, and eases the helpers' burden in reviewing them.

With Rsourcer, an ESR is assisted when elaborating their feedback request on a research draft (R1), stating their specific feedback needs (e.g., feedback on Related Work) and able to distribute the request to trusted researchers or research groups (i.e., the helpers) (R2). Helpers can collaboratively offer their feedback in the form of smaller review assignments called *micro-reviews* (R3), and rate each other micro-reviews so the most appropriate ones surface (R4). The ESR can then have access to a curated and aggregated list of reviews, structured as actionable items in a spreadsheet (R4). Further help through 1 on 1 meetings can be organised with a mentor. Rsourcer is currently offered through Slack[2] [4], which offers built-in collaboration features and it is commonly adopted by trusted newtworks (e.g., extended network of a research group, or research

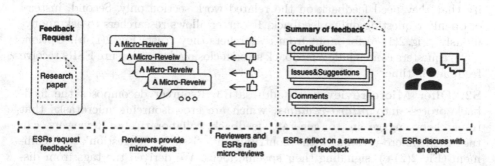

Fig. 1. Overview of the Rsourcer system.

---

[2] https://slack.com/intl/en-au/features.

community). A simplified version of this workflow is depicted in Fig. 2 and shown in higher detail in our video prototype.[3] Next, we discuss the five stages of the crowsourcing-based pipeline in detail.

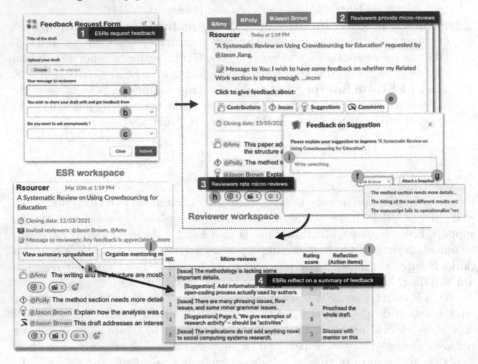

Fig. 2. Crowdsourcing-based process supported by the Rsourcer prototype in Slack.

S1: Request Feedback: To address R1 and R2, Rsourcer helps researchers form feedback requests and ensure essential information is available for reviewers [3] by providing a feedback request form (Fig. 2(1)). First, requesters can specify their needs for feedback by including a message for reviewers to focus on specific aspects of the draft(Fig. 2(1)-a). For example, requesters can specify that they need feedback on the related work section only. Second, instead of openly requesting online feedback, Rsourcer allows researchers to ask anonymously (Fig. 2(1)-c) for input from researchers they trust (Fig. 2(I)-b). Optionally, requesters can include a feedback session closing date to ensure ESRs receive feedback in time.

S2: Offer Micro-reviews: To address R3, Rsourcer decomposes the feedback process into *micro-reviews*, which are crowdsourcing microtasks that researchers engage in to generate feedback collaboratively. Reviewers can tag their micro-reviews with 'contribution', 'issue', 'suggestion', or 'comment'(Fig. 2(2)-e), signaling their specific focus. We derived the tags from discussions on what constitutes good research reviews [6]. Contributions describe

---

[3] The video prototype is available at https://bit.ly/3ZZfC9s.

the strengths and utility of the work. Issues describe problems and limitations of the work. Suggestions describe concrete changes to improve the work, such as suggestions on how to solve issues. Comments describe any other aspects that the reviewer deems relevant. Examples of micro-reviews are shown in Fig. 2(4)-i.

S3: Rate Other's Micro-reviews: To address both R3 and R4, Rsourcer allows reviewers to rate others' micro-reviews. This helps authors identify good-quality feedback [11]. Ratings also help reviewers to self-reflect and improve their future micro-reviews [1]. Micro-reviews can be rated as actionable, justified and/or specific (Fig. 2(3)-h). We adopted these criteria from the attributes of feedback on creative designs [17] and formative assessment [12]. A micro-review is actionable if it guides on improving the draft; justified if it explains the reasons for a micro-review; and specific if it is related directly to a particular part of the work.

S4: Reflect on a Summary of Feedback: To address R4, the requester can get a summary of micro-reviews and ratings of the micro-reviews. In this way, Rsourcer may help ESRs to sift through the feedback and prioritize issues to consider [16]. The summary is in the form of a spreadsheet (Fig. 2(4)-i). Ratings on micro-reviews (R_i) are presented in different colors according to quality scores (Q_i), where $Q_i = sum(R_i)/sum(R_{1-N}) * 10$. The micro-reviews are colored in green if $Q_i \geq 7$, indicating that the micro-review is rated as high quality; yellow if $4 < Q_i < 6$, indicating moderate quality; red if $Q_i \leq 4$, indicating insufficient quality. Both requester and mentors can add comments, notes and action items to the spreadsheet in the column of 'Reflection (Action Items)'.

S5: Discuss with a Mentor: To address R2 and R4, Rsourcer links authors with mentors to discuss the feedback. The requester can organize a 1–1 mentoring meeting with a volunteer expert (Fig. 2(4)-j).

3 Evaluation

3.1 Methods

We ran a preliminary assessment so as to obtain feedback on the tool and process behind our proposal. This includes a *concept validation* study guided by a video prototype to systematically obatin feedback on the features and concepts of the tool, and a *pilot study* where ESRs experienced the underlying process by relying on existing tools.

Study 1: Concept Validation. We conducted an online survey[4] [5], in which we demonstrate Rsourcer video mockups and collect quantitative and open-ended feedback on Rsourcer. We collected 48 voluntary responses till data saturation was reached [13]. The respondents include 31 (64%) ESRs in STEM and 17 (36%) ESRs in HASS. They came from Asia, Canada and USA, Europe, Latin America and Oceania.

Study 2: Pilot Study. To further evaluate Rsourcer and get in-depth qualitative feedback, we conducted a pilot study. We recruited researchers to act

---

[4] The full survey is available at http://bitly.ws/BDD9.

as requesters and helpers to use Rsourcer. Each requester asks for feedback on one of their research paper. Then, we send the papers and requests to reviewers. Each reviewer chose at least two papers (other than their own papers) and provided their micro-reviews following the Rsourcer pipeline. The micro-reviews were then sent to other reviewers and the requesters for ratings. Finally, the micro-reviews and ratings were summarised in spreadsheets and sent back to each requester. We interviewed participants about their perception of the process and how useful they perceive Rsourcer for scaling feedback. We conducted an inductive thematic analysis on the interview data [2]. We recruited nine voluntary researchers. Three participated as requesters, two as requesters and reviewers, and four as helpers. We collected 47 micro-reviews, including 7 (14%) 'contributions', 11(22%) 'issues', 20 (42%) 'suggestions' and 9 (22%) 'comments'.

3.2   Results

The **concept validation** study first inquired about current attitutes towards online feedback to researchers beyond their research groups. A 73% of the participants reported never or rarely requesting feedback, while for providing feedback the percentage went to 79%. This illustrates the extent to which the challenges from our preliminary studies affect ESR ability to obtain and provide feedback. While walking the participants throught the concept of Rsourcer and its features, they rated the usefulness of the key features in addressing the salient challenges to requesting, providing and adopting feedback. The breakdown by feature is illustrated in Fig. 3, and shows the overall positive reponse to the concepts. The with the least (relative) usefulness is tha rating of micro-reviewers, which some participants reported as complicated.

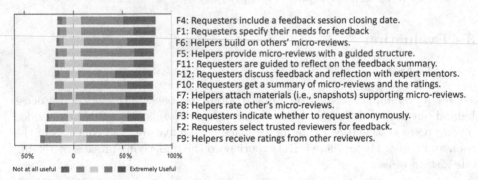

Fig. 3. Researchers' perceived usefulness of each feature (Experiment 1)

After showing the video prototype, participants were inquired about how likely their attitude towards requesting, providing and adopting feedback online will change with Rsourcer. A 82% of participants reported that they are somewhat or extremely likely to change their attitute towars requesting feedback, while that figure goes to 75% for providing feedback, and 73% for adoption feedback. Whle preliminary, these results show the potential to support ESRs in the feedback elicitation process.

The **pilot study**, along with the open-ended feedback from the concept validation study, provided a more in-depth view into the opinions and experiences of participants. We explain the findings with representative participant quotes (in italics). We denote participants from Study 1 and Study 2 as Vn and Pn.

Micro-Reviews Lower the Threshold for both Asking and Providing Feedback. With micro-reviews, participants were less concerned with adding workload to helpers and thus more willing to seek feedback. *"I often fear that I am burdening my colleagues if I ask them for feedback, especially when I send a large chunk of the paper. The ability to distribute this burden across multiple people and have them review it in small chunks (micro-reviews) is a great concept. It means I can get more feedback from more people without feeling so bad about adding to a specific person's workload."* (V5). Interestingly, one participant suggested further lowering the barrier of providing feedback by offering the helpers *"'micro context' about the paper, so I could then digest the solicited section and provide my feedback"* (V41).

A Structured Crowd-basd Pipeline has the Potential to Speed-up the Feedback Process. Rsourcer reportedly *"speed(s) up the process"* of requesting for feedback *"because it gives a structure to the process"* (V2), guiding the elaboration of requests, feedback and quality assessment. This was brought up especially by participants from the pilot study, who experiencing the process. It was particularly associated to the micro-reviews that enable them to spend much less time comparing with reviewing for journal or conference papers as they could focus on the specific feedback requests. However, the amount of effort required may depend on the type of paper and request. As one participant stated: *"The author asked only for feedback on Sect. 4, but I will have to read other sections to understand the algorithms in Sect. 4"* (P3), hinting the importance of onboarding helpers into the context (e.g., micro-contexts) as previously suggested by participant V41.

Ratings on Micro-reviews has the Potential to Improve Review Quality and Quality Assessment. With the ratings, participants find it helpful *"to improve the quality of my reviews"* as reviewers(V5). As requesters, ratings helped validate the external feedback. A requester received unfair feedback from conference reviews, *"but having ratings from other reviewers makes things different. I know whether the issues are agreed by others"* (P1). However, some respondents from both experiments were confused with the detailed rating scheme. Respondents suggested a simpler rating system: *"would rather have just a +1/thumbs down rating than the ones suggested"* (V43).

Targeted Requests have the Potential to Fulfill Specific Feedback Needs. For example, V2 mentioned that *"feedback regarding specific elements of a draft"* allow them to get *"more targeted"* feedback. Among the five feedback requests in Experiment 2, one asked for feedback on results and discussion, one on a section about algorithms, one asked about the Introduction and two asked for feedback on general aspects of the paper with an emphasis on the writing.

68   Y. Jiang et al.

References

1. Bharadwaj, A., Siangliulue, P., Marcus, A., Luther, K.: Critter: augmenting creative work with dynamic checklists, automated quality assurance, and contextual reviewer feedback. In: CHI 2019, pp. 1–12 (2019)
2. Braun, V., Clarke, V.: Successful Qualitative Research: A Practical Guide for Beginners. SAGE, Thousand Oaks (2013)
3. Cheng, R., Zeng, Z., Liu, M., Dow, S.: Critique me: exploring how creators publicly request feedback in an online critique community. In: Proceedings of the ACM on Human-Computer Interaction, vol. 4 (CSCW2), pp. 1–24 (2020)
4. Fulcher, M.R., et al.: Broadening participation in scientific conferences during the era of social distancing. Trends Microbiol. **28**(12), 949–952 (2020)
5. Greenberg, S., Buxton, B.: Usability evaluation considered harmful (some of the time). In: CHI 2008, pp. 111–120 (2008)
6. Hinckley, K.: So you're a program committee member now: on excellence in reviews and meta-reviews and championing submitted work that has merit (2015). https://bit.ly/3cCG3Pg
7. Introne, J., Semaan, B., Goggins, S.: A sociotechnical mechanism for online support provision. In: CHI 2016, pp. 3559–3571 (2016)
8. Jiang, Y.: Scaling Research Support for Early-Stage Researchers with Crowdsourcing. Ph.D. thesis, University of New South Wales (2021)
9. Jiang, Y., Báez, M., Benatallah, B.: Understanding how early-stage researchers perceive external research feedback. In: CI 2021. ACM (2021)
10. Jiang, Y., Schlagwein, D., Benatallah, B.: A review on crowdsourcing for education: state of the art of literature and practice. In: PACIS 2018 (2018)
11. Krause, M., Garncarz, T., Song, J., Gerber, E.M., Bailey, B.P., Dow, S.P.: Critique style guide: improving crowdsourced design feedback with a natural language model, pp. 4627–4639. ACM, New York, NY, USA (2017)
12. Sadler, D.R.: Formative assessment and the design of instructional systems. Instr. Sci. **18**(2), 119–144 (1989). https://doi.org/10.1007/BF00117714
13. Saunders, B., et al.: Saturation in qualitative research: exploring its conceptualization and operationalization. Qual. Q. 1–15 (2017). https://doi.org/10.1007/s11135-017-0574-8
14. Vaish, R., et al.: Crowd research: open and scalable university laboratories. In: UIST 2017, pp. 829–843. ACM, New York, NY, USA (2017)
15. Wang, T., Li, L.Y.: 'tell me what to do' vs. 'guide me through it': feedback experiences of international doctoral students. Active Learn. High. Educ. **12**(2), 101–112 (2011)
16. Yen, Y.C.G., Kim, J.O., Bailey, B.P.: Decipher: an interactive visualization tool for interpreting unstructured design feedback from multiple providers. In: CHI 2020. pp. 1–13. ACM, New York, NY, USA (2020)
17. Yuan, A., Luther, K., Krause, M., Vennix, S.I., Dow, S.P., Hartmann, B.: Almost an expert: the effects of rubrics and expertise on perceived value of crowdsourced design critiques. In: CSCW 2016, pp. 1005–1017. ACM, New York, NY, USA (2016)
18. Zhang, H., Easterday, M.W., Gerber, E.M., Lewis, D.R., Maliakal, L.: Agile research studios: orchestrating communities of practice to advance research training. In: CSCW 2017 Companion, pp. 45–48. ACM, New York, NY, USA (2017)

Predictive Recommining: Learning Relations Between Event Log Characteristics and Machine Learning Approaches for Supporting Predictive Process Monitoring

Christoph Drodt[1]([⊠]) [iD], Sven Weinzierl[2] [iD], Martin Matzner[2] [iD],
and Patrick Delfmann[1] [iD]

[1] Institute for IS Research, Universität Koblenz, Koblenz, Germany
{drodt,delfmann}@uni-koblenz.de
[2] Institute of Information Systems, Friedrich-Alexander-Universität
Erlangen-Nürnberg, Nuremberg, Germany
{sven.weinzierl,martin.matzner}@fau.de

Abstract. A variety of predictive process monitoring techniques based on machine learning (ML) have been proposed to improve the performance of operational processes. Existing techniques suggest different ML algorithms for training predictive models and are often optimized based on a small set of event logs. Consequently, practitioners face the challenge of finding an appropriate ML algorithm for a given event log. To overcome this challenge, this paper proposes *Predictive Recommining*, a framework for suggesting an ML algorithm and a sequence encoding technique for creating process predictions based on a new event log's characteristics (e.g., loops, number of traces, number of joins/splits). We show that our instantiated framework can create correct recommendations for the next activity prediction task.

Keywords: Predictive Process Monitoring · Machine Learning · Business Process Management · Process Mining · Decision Support

1 Introduction

Predictive process monitoring (PPM) provides a set of techniques addressing tasks such as predicting the next activities, process outcomes, or throughput times in running processes. Given these predictions, process stakeholders can proactively intervene to improve the performance or reduce risks of operational processes [12]. PPM uses predictive models constructed from event log data to generate predictions. In constructing a predictive model, recent PPM techniques use machine learning (ML) algorithms, which can create accurate predictions for different tasks and data sets [6]. However, plenty of new ML algorithms have been proposed for PPM, which increases the possibility of an ML algorithm fitting a given event log but complicates the selection process. Senior researchers and practitioners may rely on their experiences to suggest an ML algorithm. But this suggestion can also be wrong and misleading in finding the best matching algorithm. Typically, though, people have to conduct a time-consuming literature review and, in the best case, find evidence for an appropriate ML algorithm for a given prediction task and event log. To be more precise, an ML model's prediction performance heavily depends on the event logs' characteristics (e.g., loops, number of traces, number of joins/splits) and how well the ML algorithm can learn from event log data with these characteristics. This relation has also been observed and validated in other PPM works [4, 9, 16] and other disciplines of process mining (PM) [1, 3]. It stands to reason that this relation is also present in a predictive model, which is why we introduce *Predicitve Recommining*, a framework to suggest an ML algorithm for a given event log based on the log's characteristics. In this paper, we describe the structure of our framework and evaluate the framework with two experiments.

Therefore, this paper is structured as follows: In Sect. 2, we present our designed framework. Before Sect. 4 discusses findings, limitations, and future research directions, Sect. 3 evaluates our instantiated framework. Section 5 concludes the paper with a summary.

2   Predictive Recommining Framework

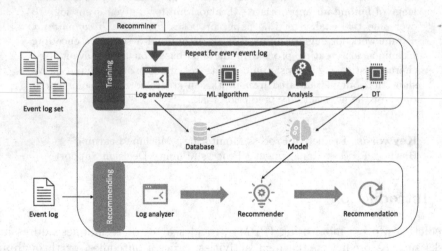

Fig. 1. Overview of the *Predictive Recommining* framework.

This framework aims to support selecting an ML algorithm and a sequence encoding technique to save time and effort in creating an accurate model for next activity prediction given a new event log. The framework is structured into an offline component, building the recommender's foundation, and an online component, applying the recommender, as shown in Fig. 1. The offline component trains and tests models using a set of ML algorithms based on a set of characteristic-diverse event logs and stores the training results in a database. Currently, five machine learning algorithms are included in the framework, that is, random forest (RF), extreme gradient boosting (XGBoost), support vector machine (SVM)[1], long short-term memory neural network (LSTM), and multilayer perceptron (MLP) [8,13–15]. Finally, this component feeds the results into a decision tree (DT)[2] algorithm to learn a model that maps the event log characteristics to the ML algorithm and the sequence encoding technique generating the most accurate next activity predictions. The online component receives the trained DT model from the offline component. The main task of this component is to recommend an ML algorithm and a sequence encoding technique based on a new event log's characteristics. The recommended ML algorithm and the sequence encoding technique can then be used to train an accurate next activity prediction model for this new event log. In the following, we detail the phases of the two components.

2.1 Offline Component: Building the Recommender

Feeding event logs into the offline component, a module we call *Log Analyzer* **reads the event logs** and **analyzes the characteristics**. This component iterates through each trace and each event of an event log, extracts all relevant information, and calculates specific metrics. These characteristics and metrics were gathered in a structured literature review [3], from which we implemented 77 characteristics out of three categories: event-log-based (37), process-model-based (32), and process-context-based (8). These categories can also be divided into sub-categories, which we listed together with the sources and a brief description in an online accessible file[3]. The returned **characteristics are stored** in a database for later processing steps.

Next, the framework pre-processes event logs, and trains and tests ML models for next activity prediction.

During the pre-processing, the framework **encodes events** of an event log, where it differentiates between attribute types (e.g. activity, time-based numerical, categorical, and numerical data).

Afterwards, the framework **encodes the sequences** of an event log, either using an index-based [10] or window-based[4] [11] technique. Finally, the framework starts training the model, where it **creates two data sets** by splitting the event log into a training (80%) and a test set (20%) on the process instance level. Before splitting, the framework does not randomly shuffle the process instances to retain their original order. This validation strategy is common in PPM research [12]. Before starting the training, the offline component can perform a hyper-parameter optimization (HPO)[5] where the training set is split

---

[1] In our case, we use a support vector classifier (SVC).
[2] For this task, any explainable ML approach can be used.
[3] https://gitlab.uni-koblenz.de/process-science/research/predictive-recommining/recomminer/-/tree/CAiSE.
[4] We set the size of the windows to 3 as recommended by [12].
[5] For detailed information about the hyper-parameter range, visit https://gitlab.uni-koblenz.de/process-science/research/predictive-recommining/recomminer.

again into a sub-training (80%) and a validation set (20%). Per default, Tree-structured Parzen Estimator as a sequential model-based optimization approach is used because it works efficiently, even in large hyperparameter spaces [2]. In the following, **models are trained** based on the pre-processed event logs. The framework can apply the included set of ML algorithms for model training because we want to recommend the most suitable for the characteristics of a new event log. After successfully training the ML models, the framework **tests the models** based on the test sets. Here, to measure the models' predictive quality, the framework calculates commonly used ML metrics (e.g., *precision*, *recall*, and *F1-score*) and **saves the metrics** in the database with a reference to the previously stored event log characteristics.

To train the recommender, the offline component **loads all necessary data** from the database gathered in the previous steps. This data is then used to **construct the DT** model with HPO — as described for constructing the ML models for the activity prediction — for the online component. The inputs for the training are the characteristics as data values and the best-performing ML algorithm and sequence encoding technique as target values.

2.2   Online Component: Applying the Recommender

Like the offline component, the online component starts with the Log Analyzer, to extract the characteristics of the given event log.

Next, the framework **loads the trained DT model**. To predict an ML algorithm and a sequence encoding technique for a given event log, the extracted **characteristics are fed** into the DT model trained in the offline component, which predicts an ML algorithm and a sequence encoding technique matching the entered characteristics. Finally, the **results are presented** to the user as a suggestion.

3   Experimental Evaluation

Details on the implementation of the framework can be obtained from [7]. To test the artifact, we designed two experiments. The first experiment tests the generalizability of the framework based on synthetic event logs. The second experiment tests the framework's ability to deal with real-world event logs. All synthetic event logs include randomly chosen activities and traces and were created using the tool PLG2 [5]. The real-world event logs considered are publicly available. All used event logs and their extracted characteristics can be found in the online repository of this paper (see Footnote 5).

In each experiment, 2/3 of the event logs are used to train the offline component (training event logs), and 1/3 are used to test the online component (test event logs). Then, each ML algorithm and sequence encoding technique are applied to all event logs from the test set to identify the best ML algorithm and sequence encoding technique. The results are compared with the recommendation from the online component. The evaluation of this comparison reveals the predictive performance of the DT model and, therefore, the recommendation performance of the framework. As stated in Sect. 2.1, the target value for training the DT model is the ML algorithm combined with the sequence encoding technique used to train the most accurate next activity prediction model.

We use different evaluation metrics for the ML models as the best ML model can differ from metric to metric. Therefore, the DT model is trained and evaluated for the best ML algorithm and sequence encoding technique for the following metrics: weighted and macro F1-score, precision, and recall.

In addition, HPO was enabled for training next activity prediction models with each ML algorithm (10 rounds) and for the training of the DT model (100 rounds) in every experiment.

3.1 Experiment I: Generalizability Test

The first experiment is designed to test the generalizability of our framework. For that, we use 60 synthetic event logs containing between 5 and 20 activities and between 102 and 3,991 traces. From these 60 event logs, we randomly select 40 event logs for training and use the remaining 20 event logs for testing.

Predictive Performance for Classification Models: Figure 2 shows that all classification models generally perform quite similarly, apart from a few outliers.[6] Especially the MLP achieves a relatively low F1-score on event log *Process8-A16-T102*. Nevertheless, we can not observe that models trained with a particular ML algorithm systematically outperform models trained with another ML algorithm across all event logs.

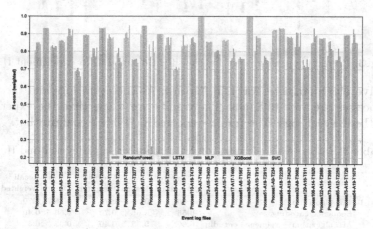

Fig. 2. Predictive performance for classification models in experiment I.

Predictive Performance for DT Model: The range of the predictions is between 30% and 70%. The lowest score for each metric is the correct prediction of both ML algorithm and sequence encoding technique (c.f. Table 1).

---

[6] For better readability, we only included in the plot the first 40 event logs. The plot that includes all 60 event logs can be found in the online repository.

3.2   Experiment II: Real-live Event Logs

In the last experiment, we apply our framework to real-life event logs. We use several publicly available event logs, available in the repository (see Footnote 5). From these eight sources, we get 21 event logs since most of them provide multiple files. In detail, we randomly select 14 event logs for training and use the remaining seven event logs for testing.

Predictive Performance for Classification Models: The performance of the classification models follows a trend for each event log; hence, in most cases, there are huge gaps between each classification model's performance (see Fig. 3). Obviously, the classification model trained with the SVM results in a score of 0.0 for some event logs. This is due to a timeout of 24 h we set for the HPO, as well as for the training process in the offline component. The SVM reached this timeout several times.

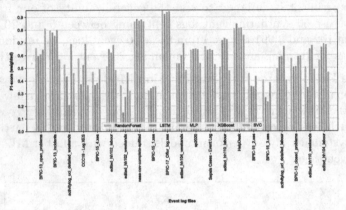

Fig. 3. Predictive performance for classification models in experiment II.

Predictive Performance for DT Model: As the event logs and the underlying processes are very different. The results are worse than the experiments with synthetic event logs. The results reported in Table 1 confirm that.

Table 1. Predictive performance for DT model in experiment I and II.

		F1-score		Precision		Recall	
		Weighted	Macro	Weighted	Macro	Weighted	Macro
Experiment I	ML algorithm	0.50	0.50	0.70	0.55	0.70	0.60
	Sequence encoding	0.55	0.65	0.70	0.60	0.40	0.50
	ML algorithm + sequence encoding	0.30	0.35	0.40	0.35	0.35	0.30
Experiment II	ML algorithm	0.28	0.14	0.42	0.42	0.28	0.42
	Sequence encoding	0.85	1.00	0.85	0.85	0.85	0.71
	ML algorithm + sequence encoding	0.25	0.14	0.42	0.42	0.28	0.28

4   Discussion

The results of the experiments reveal that the framework works and can deliver reasonable results. The suggestion performance of the offline component in the first experiment was very good and, therefore, confirms that the DT model can recall the learned behavior. In experiment I, the recommendation performance of the offline component ranged between 45% and 65% for the ML algorithms across all metrics. Considering that the training set holds more variables (77) than rows (40), which is, in general, problematic for an ML algorithm, the performance can be rated as good. In experiment II, the prediction performance of the DT model is lower than in the other experiments, which can be the result of the heterogeneous event logs (see Footnote 5). Additionally, the training set is relatively small for such a divergence, which might be an important factor for the resulting prediction performance for both experiments. Interestingly, in both experiments, no models trained with a particular algorithm systematically outperformed models trained with another algorithm in the training phase considering all performance metrics. In experiment II, for example, the SVM classification model was the best-performing model for some event logs but the worst classification model for other event logs. This supports the findings of other research teams in other PM disciplines that there is no best-performing ML algorithm and underlines the need for our framework.

As with other research, ours is not free of limitations. We implemented five ML algorithms for the offline component and two types of sequence encoding. Many other ML algorithms and sequence encoding techniques exist for next activity prediction in PPM. We did not consider these in this paper, even though they could provide more insights into the relation between the event log characteristics and the next activity prediction performance. Nevertheless, the selected ML algorithms and sequence encoding techniques are sufficiently comprehensive for the conduction of our experiments.

In future research, the selection of important event log characteristics should be further investigated. It could also be that not all characteristics are important for the recommendation process. This raises the question of whether specific characteristics are always important for the recommendation process and, therefore, the learning data for the DT can be reduced to a subset of characteristics.

5   Conclusion

This paper presented the *Predictive Recommining* framework that can recommend an ML algorithm and a sequence encoding technique for a given event log. We described the framework and explained its functionality. To evaluate the framework, we created an instantiation and conducted experiments. The results of the experiments show that the instantiated framework works and can deliver reasonable recommendations, which cut short the process of finding a suitable ML algorithm and sequence encoding technique for a given event log. The results also path the way for improving the recommendation quality in future work.

Acknowledgments. Funded by the Deutsche Forschungsgemeinschaft (DFG, German Research Foundation) - Research Grant No. 432399058 and No. 445156547

References

1. Augusto, A., Mendling, J., Vidgof, M., Wurm, B.: The connection between process complexity of event sequences and models discovered by process mining. Inf. Sci. **598**, 196–215 (2022)
2. Bergstra, J., Bardenet, R., Bengio, Y., Kégl, B.: Algorithms for hyper-parameter optimization. In: Advances in Neural Information Processing Systems, vol. 24 (2011)
3. vanden Broucke, S.K., Delvaux, C., Freitas, J., Rogova, T., Vanthienen, J., Baesens, B.: Uncovering the relationship between event log characteristics and process discovery techniques. In: Business Process Management Workshops, pp. 41–53 (2013)
4. Brunk, J., Stottmeister, J., Weinzierl, S., Matzner, M., Becker, J.: Exploring the effect of context information on deep learning business process predictions. J. Decis. Syst. **29**(sup1), 328–343 (2020)
5. Burattin, A.: PLG2: multiperspective process randomization with online and offline simulations. In: CEUR Workshop Proceedings (2016)
6. Di Francescomarino, C., Ghidini, C., Maggi, F.M., Milani, F.: Predictive process monitoring methods: which one suits me best? In: International Conference on Business Process Management, pp. 462–479 (2018)
7. Drodt, C., Weinzierl, S., Matzner, M., Delfmann, P.: The recomminder: a decision support tool for predictive business process monitoring. In: Proceedings of the Best Dissertation Award, Doctoral Consortium, and Demonstration & Resources Track at BPM 2021 co-located with 19th International Conference on Business Process Management (BPM 2021). CEUR Workshop Proceedings, vol. 2973, pp. 131–135 (2021)
8. Evermann, J., Rehse, J.R., Fettke, P.: Predicting process behaviour using deep learning. Decis. Support Syst. **100**, 129–140 (2017)
9. Heinrich, K., Zschech, P., Janiesch, C., Bonin, M.: Process data properties matter: introducing gated convolutional neural networks (GCNN) and key-value-predict attention networks (KVP) for next event prediction with deep learning. Decis. Support Syst. **143**, 113494 (2021)
10. Leontjeva, A., Conforti, R., Di Francescomarino, C., Dumas, M., Maggi, F.M.: Complex symbolic sequence encodings for predictive monitoring of business processes, pp. 297–313 (2015)
11. Márquez-Chamorro, A.E., Resinas, M., Ruiz-Cortés, A., Toro, M.: Run-time prediction of business process indicators using evolutionary decision rules. Expert Syst. Appl. **87**, 1–14 (2017)
12. Marquez-Chamorro, A.E., Resinas, M., Ruiz-Cortes, A.: Predictive monitoring of business processes: a survey. IEEE Trans. Serv. Comput. **11**(6), 962–977 (2018)
13. Senderovich, A., Di Francescomarino, C., Ghidini, C., Jorbina, K., Maggi, F.M.: Intra and inter-case features in predictive process monitoring: a tale of two dimensions. In: International Conference on Business Process Management, pp. 306–323 (2017)
14. Tama, B.A., Comuzzi, M.: An empirical comparison of classification techniques for next event prediction using business process event logs. Expert Syst. Appl. **129**, 233–245 (2019)
15. Teinemaa, I., Dumas, M., Leontjeva, A., Maggi, F.M.: Temporal stability in predictive process monitoring. Data Min. Knowl. Discovery **32**(5), 1306–1338 (2018)
16. Weinzierl, S., et al.: An empirical comparison of deep-neural-network architectures for next activity prediction using context-enriched process event logs. arXiv (2020)

A Goal-Driven Approach to Support Decision-Making with Incomplete Information in Cyber Operations

Ahmed Dawoud[1] , Geeta Mahala[2] , Chadni Islam[3] , Wolfgang Mayer[1] ,
Aditya Ghose[2] , M. Ali Babar[3] , Markus Stumptner[1](✉) ,
and Georg Grossmann[1]

[1] University of South Australia, Adelaide, Australia
{Ahmed.Dawoud,Wolfgang.Mayer,Markus.Stumptner,Georg.Grossmann}
@unisa.edu.au
[2] University of Wollongong, Wollongong, Australia
gm168@uowmail.edu.au, aditya@uow.edu.au
[3] The University of Adelaide, Adelaide, Australia
{chadni.islam,ali.babar}@adelaide.edu.au

Abstract. Semi-autonomous cyber security ("cyber") operations
require effective communication between a human operator and the
underlying cyber systems that carry out the mission. We show a goal-
driven approach to specifying mission objectives of such systems, where
the system has controlled autonomy to refine the goals into executable
plans. An ontology aligns goal decomposition and data representation
with human-level concepts, and probabilistic extensions of Belief-Desire-
Intention (BDI) agent architectures allow dealing with uncertainty about
the agent's state and the effects of its actions. Our framework effectively
automates parts of cyber operations while conveying the state of operations to a human operator. A case study from the cyber operations
domain demonstrates that this approach can outperform the traditional
BDI agent approach while requiring minimal additional information by
the agent programmer.

1 Introduction

Recent advances in Artificial Intelligence (AI) have enabled systems with greater
autonomy in decision-making. Although autonomy enables systems to respond
faster and achieve better outcomes, this poses challenges for the human observer.
A human observer must maintain situational awareness about (i) what the system is doing and (ii) the underlying reasons for automated decision outcomes to
ensure that the goals and objectives the system is pursuing align with those of the
human operator, despite perhaps only partially understanding the environment

This research was supported by the Australian Government via the Defence-funded
Next Generation Technology Fund (NGTF) in collaboration with Data61, University
of South Australia, The University of Adelaide, and the University of Wollongong.

C. Cabanillas and F. Perez (Eds.): CAiSE 2023, LNBIP 477, pp. 77–85, 2023.
https://doi.org/10.1007/978-3-031-34674-3_10

and actions. For example, in cyber security operations (commonly shortened to Cyber operations) [6], an analyst may possess expertise in interpreting information collected by an automated system; however, the details of how computer networks and related tools operate may be outside of the analyst's expertise.

Goal-based planning techniques are well-suited to devising concrete executable actions that achieve given goals. High-level goals phrased in terms of concepts familiar to the human express objectives that the system shall achieve, whereas the system devises suitable plans and executes actions to achieve the set goals.

The Belief-Desire-Intention (BDI) model [7] is a well-established approach to goal-based planning that combines an agent's belief (what it knows about the environment) with desires (what the agent wants to achieve) and intentions (decisions the agent has committed to). However, the BDI paradigm traditionally relies on a fixed library of plans in the order predetermined at design time. This can prevent the agent from devising effective plans if the planning strategy changes as more is known about the environment. For example, the means to pursue goals in cyber operations can change dramatically depending on new information about the target network and its potential vulnerabilities. Moreover, the purely reactive approach to selecting intentions in its reasoning cycle is limited as the expectations about the outcomes of future actions can influence the intention selection decisions. Extensions are needed to address these dynamic changes without requiring the BDI programmer to anticipate all possible scenarios at design time. Key research challenges that arise in this context are:

- A conceptual representation aligned with the language used by domain experts is required for conveying the state of the system to the human observer. Existing informal models of cyber operations, including the Cyber Kill Chain and MITRE frameworks, are designed only for human comprehension of individual aspects of cyber operations, but do not link those aspects. Domain ontologies capturing the key elements and data about cyber networks [8] are not integrated with the operational view of cyber operations. An integrated model is needed to be able to formulate hierarchical goals and plans that can be presented to human observers at different levels of abstraction.
- A mechanism for adopting goals and transitioning between goals is required that is effective under incomplete and uncertain information. The considerable amount of incomplete knowledge in such environments can render traditional heuristics, classical planning, and pure probabilistic transition models ineffective [2]. In Cyber operations, adversary actions usually result in uncertainty about which method have been used by an adversary, whether the target is vulnerable, and whether an exploit has already been used successfully [4]. Though learning-based approaches for selected cyber operations exist, e.g. for penetration testing [5], these methods require considerable training effort given the sparsity of reward signals in cyber operations and have limited ability to explain decisions, showing the need for hybrid alternatives [4].

We address these challenges through extensions of the BDI architecture with a domain ontology for representing the agent's belief and formulating goals and plans, and with Bayesian reasoning and Markov Decision Processes to inform the planner's decisions based on incomplete or uncertain information the agent has.

We use a Penetration Testing case study to demonstrate the approach. Penetration testing is an attack-based simulation approach used to identify and exploit vulnerabilities to evaluate the security of systems in an organization [1].

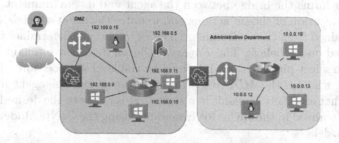

Fig. 1. Example cyber network structure.

The network scenario is shown in Fig. 1. It consists of eight hosts spread across two subnets connected by switches and routers. It is assumed that the agent (the attacker in the scenario) has compromised a host in the DMZ as an initial foothold. All information about the target network, its topology, hosts, and software systems has to be discovered via the activities driven by the BDI agent. The goal of the BDI agent is to discover a sequence of actions that allow the agent to move laterally from one subnet to another and exfiltrate confidential information from the Administrative network on the right.

2   Extended BDI Framework

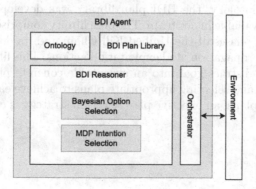

Fig. 2. Conceptual Architecture

The conceptual architecture for goal-based decision-making under uncertainty is shown in Fig. 2. An *ontology* expresses goals at an abstraction suitable for human understanding and (building on the principles in [3]) aligns them with the more detailed concepts required to describe executable actions, their preconditions, and possible effects that the machine (e.g., an agent) requires to plan and execute actions. The ontology forms the language used to construct the *BDI plan library*, which expresses goals and possible means to achieve them. The *orchestrator* forms the bridge between the agent and its environment. It orchestrates the execution of chosen actions and updates the agent's beliefs with information obtained from the environment. The *BDI reasoner* determines the agent's actions based on its beliefs. The *Bayesian Option Selection* mechanism enables the agent to select plans options informed by the level of uncertainty in the current beliefs, whereas the *MDP intention selection* guides the agent in selecting intentions that are likely to result in a state that is closer to the desired goal. Our system was realized in the JaCaMo[1] framework using the GeNIe Modeler[2] for the Bayesian model.

2.1   Cyber Domain Ontology and BDI Plan Library

Several domain-specific ontologies were obtained and aligned to define the conceptual model underlying the BDI agent framework. The modular architecture separates the information domain from the planning domain and separate multiple levels of abstraction within the planning domain. The ontology captures and formalizes the agent's capabilities aligned with selected MITRE frameworks. The model integrates goals at four levels of abstraction. The highest level corresponds to the general *tactics* part of the overall kill chain. The tactics are refined into more concrete *techniques* (based on MITRE ATT&CK), which are refined into *attack patterns* (MITRE CAPEC) that are in turn associated with *weaknesses* (MITRE CWE), which group *vulnerabilities* (CVE) that may be associated with concrete software tools exploiting the vulnerabilities. The layers form the basis for decomposing high-level goals into executable goals. Finally, the CNTFO ontology [8] captures the structures of cyber networks and their properties.

Based on the ontology, the BDI plan library was developed based on the domain expertise available in our team. The plan library comprised 31 plans which captured the main phases of the Unified Kill Chain and its decomposition into specific discovery, propagation, and exploitation actions. This library enabled the agent to refine an abstract goal into an executable concrete plan by iteratively decomposing goals and selecting appropriate plans to achieve each goal. As there are many possible plans, an effective plan selection strategy is critical.

---

[1] http://jacamo.sourceforge.net/.
[2] www.bayesfusion.com/genie/.

2.2   Plan Option Selection Under Uncertainty

At the core of the BDI paradigm lies an iterative reasoning cycle (Fig. 3) where the agent selects an event it received for processing, examines its belief base to determine which plan options may pertain to the selected event, selects an intention to pursue in this cycle, and decides which plan to select for execution.

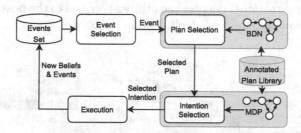

Fig. 3. Extended BDI reasoning cycle. Extension highlighted in green. (Color figure online)

An option selection mechanism selects a preferred plan among the possible plans available to the agent depending on its current belief about its intentions and the environment. Here, the context conditions associated with plans play a critical role in that only plans whose context conditions are satisfied given the belief base are considered. If the truth value of the context condition cannot be established, for example, if the beliefs are incomplete or beliefs are associated with a degree of uncertainty, a plan may either not be considered or it may be considered in situations where it is unlikely to succeed.

To deal with the kinds of uncertainty about the mission state mentioned in the introduction, our extensions introduce a probabilistic method capable of selecting options that are likely to advance the agent's goals. A Bayesian Decision Network (BDN) was created that models the dependency of major decisions the agent can make on the available information. The BDN utilises abstractions of the agent's beliefs derived from the context conditions of the plans in the agent's plan library. For each plan, the BDN computes an expectation of the success prospect the agent's beliefs and contextual conditions associated with plans and computes an expected utility associated with each plan.

A fragment of the BDN is shown in Fig. 4. The model includes a set of variables derived from the conceptual model and a set of decision nodes representing goals, subgoals, and utility nodes for each decision considering the variables, causal relationships, and the probabilities of these variables. The nodes represent either beliefs or sub-networks, and directed edges represent an effect that a parent may have on the child node in the network. The model consists of three types of nodes. The nodes adorned with yellow ovals represent the probabilistic variables with an associated probability distribution, the rectangle-adorned nodes include the decision alternatives, and the diamond-adorned nodes represent the utility values for these decisions. For example, node "User" represents if the agent has compromised a user account on the current host that has either normal or superuser privileges. If that information is known in the agent's belief base, the value of that node is set; otherwise, a probabilistic estimation is used to identify the likelihood of that being the case. In Fig. 4, the node labelled *Vul* is set to the belief the agent has, whereas the remaining probabilistic variables for *User* and *VulSeverit* are not precisely known by the agent and hence represented as distributions. The node *NetworkPropagationU* denotes the utilities ascribed to the possible decisions in the *Propagation* decision node (collapsed in the figure).

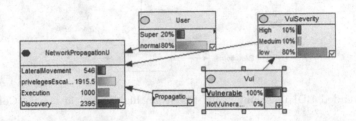

Fig. 4. A fragment of the BDN model

Using a BDN, it is possible to account for the uncertainty in the agent's beliefs, whereby some information may be unknown or known only with some degree of confidence. The BDN captures the dependency of each plan on information and uses that information to compute relative utilities of alternate plan options given the information that is currently known by an agent. The utilities are then used to select the option with maximum utility. In Fig. 4, the agent has uncertainty about the user access it has obtained and the severity of any vulnerability that may be associated with a target system. Moreover, it is currently pursuing the goal of Propagation (a phase of cyber operations), which includes the four alternative subgoals shown in node *NetworkPropagationU*. The agent would pursue *Discovery* as it is associated with the highest utility.

2.3   Intention Selection Using MDPs

An agent may face multiple (possibly competing) intentions, and it must decide which of the intentions to pursue in the current reasoning cycle. We consider outcome uncertainty in the intention selection, whereby the possible cumulative effects of a *sequence* of actions are considered in the selection process. By looking ahead, the agent can select plans whose ultimate outcomes reduce the "gap" between the actual state the agent may find itself in and the desired state in which all goals are fulfilled. This proximity can be measured using the Levenshtein-, the Dalal-, and the Hamming distance.

Our extensions rely on annotations associated with each action defined in the plan library, which express the effects that would be achieved independently of the preceding actions. Given the annotations for individual actions, the effects associated with sequences and more abstract layers in the ontology can be inferred automatically. Specifically, the possible effects of sequences of actions can be inferred by considering the possible subsets of outcomes while considering that some actions may not succeed. The resulting set of possible effects for each plan can then be used to infer the likely effects of the goals in the higher levels of abstraction in the ontology. Specifically, we adopt a reasoning framework where the common effects are retained at the abstract level.

Once the effects of actions and goals are captured, the intention selection aspect of the BDI framework reduces to a Markov Decision Problem. We characterize the states of the underlying transition system by the effects that the agent has achieved. The transitions between states are given by the actions defined in the BDI plan library, and the transition probabilities can be obtained through annotations in the plan library or, in the absence of further information, by default values. The reward associated with each state is derived from the state's proximity to the nearest goal state (where all goals are satisfied). In our prototype, the proximity is given by the differences in goals satisfied as measured by the Hamming Distance, with the reward being higher if more goals are satisfied.

This MDP can be solved using value iteration techniques to infer the optimal policy. The policy is subsequently used to select among the available intentions in the BDI agent. Hence, the solutions to the MDP guide the BDI agent towards intentions that are more likely to result in a state closer to the ideal goal state, even if the immediate next action may result in no improvement or an apparent deviation from the goal. Such situations are common in Cyber Operations where the feedback in terms of reward is often not apparent until an (often large) number of steps have been executed, and the desired effect has been achieved.

3   Execution on the Penetration Testing Case Study

We return to the case study from Fig. 1 to show the execution of the approach. Remember that the goal of the BDI agent is to find a sequence of actions to move between subnets and exfiltrate confidential information from the "inner" one.

Initially, the agent selects network propagation based on the current plan utilities, followed by a privilege escalation action (for propagation, the agent has discovery, privileges escalation, and lateral movement). After executing the privilege escalation action, the agent elects to perform network propagation again. Next, the agent selects discovery over the other possible goals (privileges escalation and lateral movement), since it already has a superuser account and a low possibility for lateral movement. The agent subsequently performs further discovery actions. In each cycle, the agent picks the discovery option with the highest utility based on the current beliefs. Initially, the agent favours host discovery over ports and service footprinting, as identifying the new hosts in the target network is required before port scanning and services footprinting can commence. During discovery, the probability of vulnerability and the severity of that vulnerability change, which increases the utility of the lateral movement activity on host 192.168.0.11. The agent selects an exploit vulnerability action to move to the host, and once it has been compromised, the agent again pursues network propagation, privileges escalation, discovery, and lateral movements to the target host 10.0.0.13. Once that host is compromised, the agent finds and exfiltrates the targeted data, after a total of 47 steps in this example.

To demonstrate the effects of the BDN- and MDP-based selection mechanisms, the same scenario was repeated with both extensions disabled. As a result, the agent was unable to complete the network propagation phase of the kill chain. These results demonstrate that the introduction of the extensions proposed in this paper can achieve significantly better results than the naive methods.

4   Conclusion

We presented a modified BDI agent architecture for acting in situations where the agent's beliefs may be incomplete, embedded in a conceptual framework where a modular ontology permits high-level goal formulation of mission objectives that are then refined into executable BDI plans. We proposed extensions to the BDI reasoning cycle whereby a Bayesian network-based mechanism for estimating the missing parts of the incomplete beliefs of an agent enabled us to select applicable plans under incomplete information, and a probabilistic intention selection mechanism aimed to guide the agent towards states that satisfy more goals. We demonstrated the effectiveness of the extensions in a Cyber Operations scenario, an exemplary setting where semi-autonomous operations will be necessary to deal with large, changing problem spaces, but high-level interaction with the human operator should be maintained at the goal level.

Further work will be directed at extending the approach to additional case studies and incorporating assumptions about the environment the agent may generate and utilize at the different levels of abstraction in the decision-making process, further demonstrating the Cyber-Human interaction in mission execution.

References

1. Denis, M., Zena, C., Hayajneh, T.: Penetration testing: concepts, attack methods, and defense strategies. In: 2016 IEEE Long Island Systems, Applications and Technology Conference (LISAT), pp. 1–6. IEEE (2016)
2. Hoffmann, J.: Simulated penetration testing: from "Dijkstra" to "Turing Test++". In: Proceedings of ICAPS, pp. 364–372 (2015)
3. Islam, C., Babar, M.A., Nepal, S.: Automated interpretation and integration of security tools using semantic knowledge. In: Proceedings of CAiSE 2019, pp. 513–528 (2019)
4. Miller, D., Alford, R., Applebaum, A., Foster, H., Little, C., Strom, B.: Automated adversary emulation: a case for planning and acting with unknowns p. 9 (2018)
5. Nguyen, H.V., Teerakanok, S., Inomata, A., Uehara, T.: The proposal of double agent architecture using actor-critic algorithm for penetration testing. In: ICISSP, pp. 440–449 (2021)

6. Randhawa, S., Turnbull, B., Yuen, J., Dean, J.: Mission-centric automated cyber red teaming. In: Proceedings of 13th International Conference on Availability, Reliability and Security, pp. 1–11 (2018)

7. Rao, A.S., Georgeff, M.P., et al.: BDI agents: from theory to practice. In: Proceedings of ICMAS, pp. 312–319 (1995)

8. Sikos, L.F., Philp, D., Howard, C., Voigt, S., Stumptner, M., Mayer, W.: Knowledge representation of network semantics for reasoning-powered cyber-situational awareness. In: Sikos, L.F. (ed.) AI in Cybersecurity. ISRL, vol. 151, pp. 19–45. Springer, Cham (2019). https://doi.org/10.1007/978-3-319-98842-9_2

Integrating IoT-Driven Events
into Business Processes

Yusuf Kirikkayis[1]([✉]) [iD], Florian Gallik[1] [iD], Ronny Seiger[2] [iD],
and Manfred Reichert[1] [iD]

[1] Institute of Databases and Information Systems, Ulm University, Ulm, Germany
{yusuf.kirikkayis,florian-1.gallik,manfred.reichert}@uni-ulm.de
[2] Institute of Computer Science, University of St.Gallen, St.Gallen, Switzerland
ronny.seiger@unisg.ch

Abstract. Extending Business Process Management (BPM) with Internet of Things (IoT) enhances process automation, improves process monitoring, and enables decision making based on data from the physical world. In this context, the transformation of low-level IoT data to process-level *IoT-driven* events constitutes an important step. However, the modeling of these transformations is challenging due to the complexity of IoT environments. Contemporary approaches do not provide sufficient support to model these transformations. Process models either become too complex with increasing numbers of devices and transformations, or this logic is externalized and viewed as a black box. This paper presents an integrated approach to model IoT-driven events in processes based on a BPMN 2.0 extension and a tool that adopts concepts from DMN. A scenario from smart production is used to demonstrate the application and improved integration of IoT-driven events in processes.

Keywords: Internet of Things · Event-driven Systems · Business Processes · Decision Modeling

1 Introduction

The interest and relevance of the Internet of Things (IoT) has increased continuously in recent years [4,8]. Sensors allow collecting data about the physical world and actuators are used to control it [1]. In turn, BPM enables the modeling, execution, monitoring, and analysis of business processes. Integrating IoT capabilities with BPM provides a more comprehensive view on business processes enhanced with data from the physical world [10]. In general, the collection of IoT data proceeds as follows: (i) sensing low-level data from the physical world, (ii) aggregating this low-level data into high-level information, and (iii) obtaining information that enables decision making in business processes [9,16]. In this work, we focus on *events* in business processes that are triggered based on the processing and abstraction of low-level IoT data.

Using standard elements for modeling IoT-driven behavior in processes has its limitations, as process model complexity increases with the number of IoT

C. Cabanillas and F. Perez (Eds.): CAiSE 2023, LNBIP 477, pp. 86–94, 2023.
https://doi.org/10.1007/978-3-031-34674-3_11

devices and their relations [7]. Decision tables provide a partial remedy here, but they cannot be directly associated with events in processes [7]. Moreover, IoT devices are treated as any other data source without being highlighted as special entities. Many approaches use BPMN 2.0 with extensions for IoT-related sensing and actuation [17]. However, the explicit integration of logic related to deriving IoT-driven process events from low-level data in processes has only been considered to a limited degree. Alternative approaches use Complex Event Processing (CEP) techniques to aggregate IoT data into process-level events based on external formalisms and tooling [2,15,16,19]. In this work, we present an approach for an integrated modeling of IoT-driven events in processes based on an extension of BPMN 2.0. This extension enables associating DMN concepts with events and allows for a seamless integration with business processes.

This paper is organized as follows: Sect. 2 introduces the problem statement and a motivating example. Section 3 discusses related work. Section 4 outlines the research method and requirements. Section 5 presents our proposal for modeling IoT-driven events in processes. Section 6 discusses our findings. Section 7 concludes the paper and presents future work.

2   Problem Statement and Motivating Example

The IoT introduces a plethora of new data sources that can be leveraged for real-time decision making in business processes [8]. Sensors and actuators produce streams of data at various levels of granularity. Using these new data sources inside a business process requires means for transforming IoT data into process-level events. These transformations should be made transparent to the process modeler. BPMN 2.0 provides various elements that may be used here, e.g., events or gateways [7]. These elements can be complemented by DMN models, which support the specification of decision tables that can be used for transformation of low-level input into high-level output [7]. To assess the suitability of BPMN 2.0 for modeling IoT-driven behavior, we have modeled a process from smart manufacturing that relies heavily on sensor events to derive process-level events. Figure 1 shows a combination of gateways, conditional events and a black box high-level event derived via CEP [15] to define IoT-driven behavior in a process.

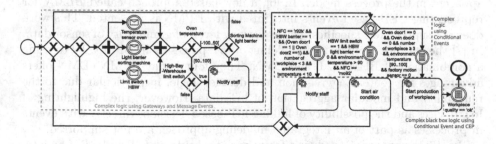

Fig. 1. IoT-Driven behavior in a smart factory modeled using BPMN 2.0

Example: Smart Manufacturing. The state of a Smart Factory is derived from a combination of sensors (temperature, light barriers, limit switches, NFC readers) using gateways and conditional events. If the factory has entered state *ready* (rightmost branch), task *Start production of workpiece* is executed. Otherwise, either *Start air condition* or *Notify staff* in case of an error are executed. After production, the quality of the workpiece is checked using an external CEP system and a conditional event *(Workpiece quality == 'ok')* [15].

The example shows that using BPMN 2.0 for modeling IoT-driven behavior comes with several disadvantages. The complexity of conditions and the high number of involved sensors in typical IoT scenarios [8] make the process model hard to understand and error-prone. Adding new sensors and conditions increases model complexity [10]. DMN could be used as a mitigation [7]. However decision tables can only be associated with *tasks* and not with *events*. The CEP-based approaches (e.g., [2,15]) are not integrated with the BPM systems. Moreover, both the BPMN+DMN and CEP approaches do not distinguish between IoT devices and other data sources [10]. This, however, is important for monitoring and error handling as the IoT devices are the links with the physical world [8].

3   Related Work

Several approaches and (extensions of) notations were proposed for representing IoT devices and IoT-related behavior in process models using specific IoT-related tasks and pools for physical entities [4,5,11,12,18]. These works propose to use dedicated process elements to represent IoT sensors and their data. As shown in the example (cf. Sect. 2), this does not scale well and becomes confusing with increasing numbers of sensors and complexity of decisions and conditions related to events. In contrast to considering individual IoT devices, approaches exist that apply CEP for sensor event aggregation and abstraction in processes [2,15,16]). While CEP is very powerful here, it usually relies on a dedicated language and external tooling to specify event processing applications. These are then only represented as black boxes in business processes. Baumgraß et al. present in [2] an approach in which they annotate process models based on a BPMN 2.0 extension to relate to events from IoT devices and convert them into higher level events. However, neither the IoT involvement nor the composition of these events are apparent in the process model. In [6], a flow-based approach called *BEMN* for representing CEP-based events integrated with BPMN is presented. This work does not support IoT specifics such as varying levels of granularity of sensor data. In [7] the authors compare the modeling of IoT processes in BPMN 2.0 to using a combination of BPMN 2.0 and DMN. They found that BPMN+DMN offers advantages for context aggregation and decision logic, in particular due to the reusability and modular aggregation of IoT data. However, the highlighting of IoT devices and the possibility of linking IoT-based decisions directly with events in processes as part of an integrated modeling approach are not supported.

In [17] the authors introduce a framework for bridging IoT and BPM by integrating IoT devices into context ontologies with the goal of improving business process decision making. They use *Business Rule Tasks* in combination with *Data Objects* for representing the IoT devices. However, these tasks are not suitable for implementing event-driven behavior within processes. In a follow-up, the authors present an approach for modeling of 1) business processes, 2) IoT devices and 3) sensor processing using different languages [19]. They argue that this separation of concerns can be beneficial for the different roles of modelers. However, they also conclude that having three different types of languages introduces high workload for modelers due to the required language familiarity.

In summary, none of the discussed approaches provides a comprehensive approach to allow an integrated modeling of complex transformations associated with events derived from IoT in a business process. Existing work either relies on external tools and languages to specify the transformations; or it only supports rather simple decision logic inside business processes considering IoT devices as any other data source. The goal of our work is to address these weaknesses and propose an integrated modeling of IoT-driven events in business processes.

4 Research Method and Requirements

The integration of IoT-driven events into business processes is a rather complex task that is related to the entire BPM lifecycle. The goal of this paper is to focus on the *modeling* of IoT-driven process events based on following research question: *How can IoT-driven events be represented in a business process model?*

Our investigation of this question follows the DSRM [13]. The problem and requirements (**R1**–**R4**) definition are based on literature (cf. Sect. 3, [8,10]) and our hands-on experience with implementing event-driven behavior in IoT-aware processes [9,14,15]. The developed artifacts comprise an extension to a modeling language and a visual notation (cf. Sect. 5). These are discussed (cf. Sect. 6) and demonstrated in a tool based on real-world examples.

R1 It shall be possible to specify event-driven behavior based on IoT data at various points in a business process. Events triggered from an external source are common in processes. IoT shall also be considered here [8]. The potentially high number of IoT devices contributing to the event-driven behavior may result in complex event specifications. It shall be possible to reuse these specifications.

R2 It shall be possible to consider IoT data from different sources and of different abstraction levels. In the smart factory, data ranges from states of motors or switches to production states [15]. It shall be possible to raise abstraction levels and to combine with data from other sources to specify event-driven behavior.

R3 The IoT devices involved in the event-driven behavior shall be treated as special data sources since they represent the interactions with the physical world. This is for example important for monitoring and error localization [8].

R4 The event-driven aspects related to IoT in a process should be specified as part of the process. They are very likely specified by the same process engineer who is familiar with the process modeling language. Instead of relying on external formalisms [15,19], IoT-driven events shall be modeled together with the process.

5 Modeling IoT-Driven Events in Processes

We use BPMN 2.0 for modeling IoT-driven process events since it is a widely adopted industry standard that supports a rich *event* concept, which we can base our extensions on. As BPMN 2.0 has several drawbacks for modeling complex transformations related to IoT data (cf. Sect. 2), we extend the language with new elements to model IoT-driven events addressing **R1**–**R3**. We first describe the extensions of the meta-model (*Abstract Syntax*) and then provide a specific example model using our proposal for the *Concrete Syntax* addressing **R4** [3].

5.1 Abstract Syntax: IoT-Driven Events in BPMN 2.0

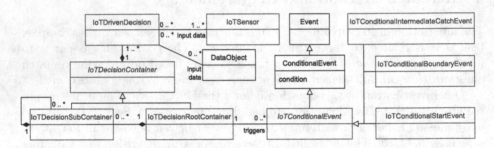

Fig. 2. BPMN 2.0 extension with IoT-related classes for events in UML

Figure 2 shows our proposal of an extension of the *Event* class of the BPMN 2.0 meta-model. Since the low-level events from IoT are intended to *drive* the execution of processes based on specific conditions, we have extended the *ConditionalEvent* with a new subclass called *IoTConditionalEvent* (**R1**), which features similar new subclasses as the original Conditional Event class. Each IoT Conditional Event is associated with one *IoTDecisionRootContainer* that may contain subcontainers (**R2**). These containers include transformations in the form of *Decisions* referring to *IoTSensors* (**R3**) and other data objects.

IoT Decision Containers contain the transformation logic represented as IoT-driven decisions [7] to derive higher level events from low-level IoT data. Thereby, the container hierarchy represents the increasing abstraction levels from lower to higher level events (**R2**). The root container triggers the IoT Conditional Event it is associated with upon the evaluation of the root container's output in the event's condition (cf. Fig. 3). Since DMN already provides means for modeling decisions in processes in the context of IoT [7], we base the meta-model within an IoT Decision Container on DMN. This allows us to define multiple IoT driven decisions inside decision tables for deriving higher level events as outputs from combinations of low-level IoT events as input. The output can serve as inputs in other decision containers or in the process (**R1**). For defining conditions we currently support standard comparison operators for single sensor values and logical operators (*AND/OR*) to combine conditions in one decision rule (**R2**).

5.2 Concrete Syntax: Visual Representation of IoT-Driven Events

Figure 3 shows the visual representation of a business process related to the smart manufacturing example. The process model created with our tool[1] contains two *IoT Conditional Intermediate Catch Events* to check the smart factory status and decide the next steps based on the specified event conditions (*Factory Status == 'ready'* or *Factory Status == 'error'*). These IoT-driven events represent decisions that depend on multiple IoT sensors (**R3**). They are connected with one *IoT Decision Root Container* that has *Factory Status* as specified output. We decided to adopt a flow-based approach [6] to model the contents of a decision container instead of using *classical* decision tables as we aim at the integration of modeling decisions and processes (**R4**). However, a translation of a decision container to a DMN table is possible. The example also shows the nesting of containers (**R2**) and the reuse of subcontainer outputs (**R1**). Subcontainers can be expanded to show details (*Heating Status*) or collapsed (*Robot Status*).

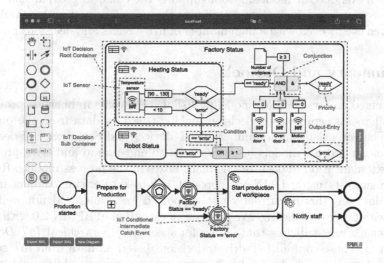

Fig. 3. Example of two IoT-driven events with an attached decision container.

6 Discussion

The research question guiding this work is referring to the representation of IoT-driven events in business process (cf. Sect. 4). From this question, we derived a

---

[1] https://github.com/elmurd0r/iot-event-modeler.

first set of requirements **R1**–**R4** that a modeling approach for IoT-driven events integrated with business processes should address. With the proposed extension of the *Conditonal Event* of BPMN 2.0 we are able to specify event-driven behavior at various points in a business process (**R1**). The event conditions are evaluated based on the outcome of the novel concept of *IoT Decision Containers* associated with the event. By nesting of decision containers, the process modeler is able to represent transformations of available IoT data to higher level container outputs on different abstraction levels and to reuse these outputs in other containers (**R2**). The expressiveness of rules and transformations inside a container is based on DMN [7]. The support for CEP-based queries in the meta-model can be achieved based on [2]. The visual modeling can be partially adapted from [6]. With **R3** we identified the need to demarcate IoT-based data sources from other process inputs for monitoring and error handling [8]. The IoT sensors are represented as first class citizens in both the proposed abstract syntax and concrete syntax. This should make their involvement in transformations and decisions related to process events clear to the end-users. We will investigate this aspect in a follow-up user study where we will also compare different approaches regarding the modeling of IoT-driven events in processes (**R4**) using our flow-based approach, BPMN+DMN [7], and query languages [2,19]. With our flow-based approach, we expect that process modelers that are already familiar with the graphical BPMN syntax should have a relatively low taskload when modeling IoT-driven events. Our modeling tool supports the collapsing/expansion of IoT decision containers, which should facilitate the modeling and understanding of IoT-driven events even with a high number of IoT devices and decisions involved.

7   Summary and Outlook

We presented an approach for modeling IoT-driven events in business processes, which allows for representing decision making based on data from the physical world. The potentially high number of IoT devices and complexity of decisions lead to either process models becoming hard to understand and error-prone, or to the externalization of decisions as black boxes in the process models. Related research suggests using DMN to represent IoT-based decision making in processes. However, this is currently not supported for events and not well integrated with process modeling. We propose an extension of BPMN 2.0 with a new *Conditional Event* subclass that allows for specifying hierarchical *IoT Decision Containers*. These contain IoT-driven decisions based on data from IoT sensors that transform data into higher level output, which can be flexibly combined and reused in other containers. The proposal for visually modeling these containers is based on a flow-oriented approach that uses similar concepts as the business process to facilitate a more seamless and improved modeling experience. We used an example process from smart manufacturing to demonstrate the applicability of the approach for modeling IoT-driven events in business processes.

In future work, we will conduct case studies in various IoT domains to validate the broad applicability of the modeling approach. Furthermore, we will conduct a user study with domain experts to evaluate the usability of the modeling concepts and tool. We will further investigate the integration of CEP to enable advanced real-time streaming data analysis for IoT-driven events and we will also consider other phases of the BPM lifecycle (e.g., implementation and monitoring).

References

1. Bauer, M., et al.: Iot reference model. In: Enabling Things to Talk, pp. 113–162. Springer, Berlin, Heidelberg (2013). https://doi.org/10.1007/978-3-642-40403-0_7
2. Baumgraß, Anne, Botezatu, Mirela, Di Ciccio, Claudio, Dijkman, Remco, Grefen, Paul, Hewelt, Marcin, Mendling, Jan, Meyer, Andreas, Pourmirza, Shaya, Völzer, Hagen: Towards a methodology for the engineering of event-driven process applications. In: Reichert, Manfred, Reijers, Hajo A.. (eds.) BPM 2015. LNBIP, vol. 256, pp. 501–514. Springer, Cham (2016). https://doi.org/10.1007/978-3-319-42887-1_40
3. Braun, R., Esswein, W.: Towards an integrated method for the extension of MOF-based modeling languages. In: Model and Data Engineering, pp. 103–115 (2015)
4. Chang, C., Srirama, S.N., Buyya, R.: Mobile cloud business process management system for the internet of things: A survey. ACM Comput. Surv. **49**(4) (2016)
5. Cheng, Y., Zhao, S., Cheng, B., Chen, X., Chen, J.: Modeling and deploying IoT-aware business process applications in sensor networks. Sensors **19**(1), 111 (2018)
6. Decker, G., Grosskopf, A., Barros, A.: A graphical notation for modeling complex events in business processes. In: 11th IEEE International Enterprise Distributed Object Computing Conference (EDOC 2007) (2007)
7. Hasić, F., Serral, E., Snoeck, M.: Comparing bpmn to BPMN + DMN for IoT process modelling: a case-based inquiry. In: Proceedings of the 35th Annual ACM Symposium on Applied Computing. p. 53–60. SAC 2020, ACM (2020)
8. Janiesch, C., et al.: The internet of things meets business process management: a manifesto. IEEE Syst. Man Cybernet. Mag. **6**(4), 34–44 (2020)
9. Kirikkayis, Y., Gallik, F., Reichert, M.: Iotdm4bpmn: an IoT-enhanced decision making framework for BPMN 2.0. In: 2022 ICSS, pp. 88–95 (2022)
10. Kirikkayis, Y., Gallik, F., Reichert, M.: Modeling, executing and monitoring iot-driven business rules with bpmn and dmn: Current support and challenges. In: Enterprise Design. Operations, and Computing, pp. 111–127. Springer, Cham (2022).https://doi.org/10.1007/978-3-031-17604-3_7
11. Martins, F., Domingos, D.: Modelling IoT behavior within BPMN business processes. Comput. Sci. **121**, 1014–1022 (2017)
12. Meyer, S., Ruppen, A., Hilty, L.: The things of the internet of things in BPMN. In: Advanced Information Systems Engineering Workshops, pp. 285–297 (2015)
13. Peffers, K., Tuunanen, T., Rothenberger, M.A., Chatterjee, S.: A design science research methodology for information systems research. J. Manag. Inf. Syst. **24**(3), 45–77 (2007)
14. Seiger, R., Assmann, U., Huber, S.: A case study for workflow-based automation in the internet of things. In: 2018 IEEE International Conference on Software Architecture Companion (ICSA-C). pp. 11–18 (2018)
15. Seiger, R., Malburg, L., Weber, B., Bergmann, R.: Integrating process management and event processing in smart factories: a systems architecture and use cases. J. Manuf. Syst. **63**, 575–592 (2022)

16. Soffer, P., et al.: From event streams to process models and back: challenges and opportunities. Inf Sys **81**, 181–200 (2019)
17. Song, R., Vanthienen, J., Cui, W., Wang, Y., Huang, L.: Context-aware bpm using iot-integrated context ontologies and iot-enhanced decision models. In: 2019 IEEE 21st Conf on Business Informatics (CBI). vol. 01, pp. 541–550 (2019)
18. Torres, V., Serral, E., Valderas, P., Pelechano, V., Grefen, P.: Modeling of IoT devices in business processes: a systematic mapping study. In: 22nd Conference on Business Informatics (CBI), vol. 1, pp. 221–230. IEEE (2020)
19. Valderas, P., Torres, V., Serral, E.: Towards an interdisciplinary development of IOT-enhanced business processes. Bus. Inf. Syst. Eng. **65**, 1–24 (2022)

Adaptive Task-Oriented Chatbots Using Feature-Based Knowledge Bases

Carla Campàs[1], Quim Motger[1]([✉]), Xavier Franch[1], and Jordi Marco[2]

[1] Department of Service and Information System Engineering, Universitat
Politècnica de Catalunya, Barcelona, Spain
carla.campas@upc.edu, {jmotger,franch}@essi.upc.edu
[2] Department of Computer Science, Universitat Politècnica de Catalunya,
Barcelona, Spain
jmarco@cs.upc.edu

Abstract. Task-oriented chatbots relying on a knowledge base for
domain-specific content exploitation have been largely addressed in
research and industry applications. Despite this, multiple challenges
remain to be fully conquered, including adaptive knowledge mechanisms,
personalization for user-specific demands, and composite intent resolution. To address these challenges, in this paper, we present a work-in-
progress summary of a task-oriented, knowledge-based chatbot in the
field of mobile software ecosystems. The chatbot is designed to assist
users in the combined use of multiple features from different applications. The proposed knowledge base and the machine learning pipeline
supporting the chatbot technical core are designed to: (i) effectively use
user context, (ii) process runtime feedback, (iii) use user historical data,
and (iv) automatically infer slot values and dependent actions. With this
report, we expect to lay the groundwork for future development stages
and user validation studies.

Keywords: Natural Language Understanding · Chatbots · Mobile
Feature Integration · Adaptive Knowledge Bases

1 Introduction

Knowledge-based dialogue systems (i.e., chatbots) define content-based interactions with users through the integration of multiple, heterogeneous data repositories to build a centralized information system (i.e., a knowledge base) for a
given domain [10]. Overall, this knowledge bases support: (1) entity linking or
extraction (i.e., the relation between entity mentions in user utterances and their
corresponding entities in the knowledge base), and (2) intent classification (i.e.,
the relation between user requests and the resources or entities in the knowledge
base that the chatbot can use to generate an appropriate response). While both
of these tasks have been intensively addressed in the Natural Language Understanding (NLU) field, several challenges remain yet to be fully conquered. In the
field of task-oriented chatbots (i.e., designed to execute a particular action from

C. Cabanillas and F. Perez (Eds.): CAiSE 2023, LNBIP 477, pp. 95–102, 2023.
https://doi.org/10.1007/978-3-031-34674-3_12

a known sub-set of pre-configured tasks [6]), one of the main challenges is the design of adaptive, personalized knowledge bases modelling the unique needs of a user, in order to provide a customized (and therefore, enhanced) experience when interacting with the chatbot [1]. Effective use of the user context, processing runtime feedback, and accessing user historical data can enact updates in the knowledge base by modelling the extracted knowledge into its entities and relations. Another significant challenge is the recognition of composite user intents, where a single intent is decomposed into multiple actions and requires extended knowledge generation to complete and respond to a specific user utterance [7]. In this case, the information embedded in the knowledge base can be used to infer slot values (i.e., entity values for a parameterized intent) and dependent actions (i.e., subsequent requests to third-party software systems) [2].

In this paper, we address these challenges by presenting the design and initial implementation stages of a knowledge-based, task-oriented dialogue system in mobile software ecosystems. Through an adapted design science research method, we address the following research question: **RQ. How task-oriented, knowledge-based chatbots can effectively and efficiently integrate adaptive, personalization, and feedback-aware mechanisms?** The resulting chatbot is designed to consume a knowledge base modelling a catalog of mobile apps, the set of functionalities (i.e., features) these apps expose, and the parameters (i.e., data items) used and generated by these features. Its main goal is to provide an adaptive, customizable experience to end users in the execution and integration of these features. Overall, this research aims at laying the groundwork for future research in the field of adaptive, context-aware, and personalized generation of knowledge-based, task-oriented dialogue systems.

2   Conceptual Model and Knowledge Base

Figure 1 presents a high-level instance of the conceptual model for mobile software ecosystems used to design the chatbot knowledge base. This model is a feature-oriented extension of the mobile software ecosystem model as defined in [9]. We briefly describe each entity, how they relate to each other, and how these concepts align with the challenges and research proposal (see Sect. 3).

- **User.** An individual end-user of a mobile device (e.g., *Alice*).
- **App.** A mobile-based software application (e.g., *Strava*). The set of apps used by a single user is what constitutes their own application portfolio (e.g., Alice's portfolio is composed of Strava and Google Calendar).
- **Feature.** A functional requirement (from the user perspective) exposed by an app (e.g., *PlanRoute*). A single feature can be exposed by multiple apps (e.g., *ScheduleEvent* is exposed by Google Calendar and Simple Calendar).
- **Parameter.** A type-based attribute defining a property-value pair for a given feature (e.g., *start-location* in *PlanRoute*).
- **Feature Integration.** A combined, semi-automatic use of two independent features (e.g., *PlanRoute-ScheduleMeeting*), defined by the integration of a

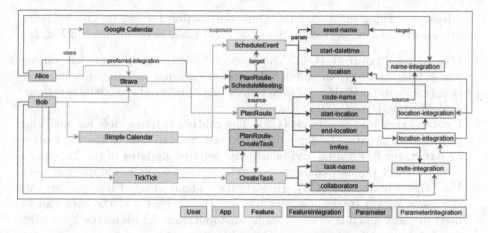

Fig. 1. Example instance of the knowledge base

source feature (e.g., *PlanRoute*), which acts as a trigger for the feature integration, and a *target* feature (e.g., *ScheduleMeeting*), which acts as the outcome, automated enacted feature based on the trigger feature. A feature integration facilitates a user's combined use of multiple features to achieve a major, complex goal. For instance, when Alice plans a route with the Strava app, the system supports scheduling an event with the Google Calendar app. This feature integration proposal is user-dependent, which means that each user defines their own *preferred-integration* relations between a source feature and a target feature between two specific apps in their own portfolio. For instance, Alice might schedule an event in Google Calendar from a newly planned route in Strava, while Bob might not only create an event in a different app from his own portfolio (e.g., Simple Calendar), but also he might create a new task with another app (e.g., TickTick).

– **Parameter Integration.** Implementation of a parameter-based integration between a source feature parameter (e.g., *start-location* from *PlanRoute*), and a target feature parameter (e.g., *location* from *ScheduleEvent*). A parameter integration facilitates to users the exchange of required data between multiple features to enact a feature integration.

The main goal of the chatbot is to act as a facilitator on the integration of features defined by the conceptual model. Through dialogue-based communication, the chatbot consumes the knowledge base to (1) trigger the corresponding feature, (2) adapt and customize the conversation with users according to their preferences, (3) collect additional, missing data from the user to run the feature, and (4) to enact any required updates to the instance knowledge-based.

3   Chatbot Story Design

To illustrate the chatbot's expected behaviour, we design a set of stories (i.e., a conversation scenario between the user and the chatbot) composing the dialogue management module. Our contribution focuses on the following design dimensions, supported by the knowledge base, as exemplified in Fig. 1:

1. **Use of user context (C1).** The proposed knowledge base models various context dimensions from mobile software ecosystems, including user information (e.g., app portfolio) and preferences (e.g., preferred feature integrations) as defined by Daniel (2018).
2. **Process runtime feedback (C2).** The chatbot is responsible for analysing positive and negative feedback from the user to start/stop a specific feature or parameter integration and enact any required updates in the knowledge base to reflect the user context and preferences (e.g., preferred integrations).
3. **Use historical data (C3).** Historic data about enacted integrations and the conversation tracker history between the chatbot and the user can be used to query and adapt user-specific customization details on the knowledge base. Additionally, the conversation history can be used to re-train entity extraction and intent recognition tasks.
4. **Infer parameter (slot) values and dependent actions (C4).** Either through preferred parameter and feature integrations modelled by the knowledge base or through traditional slot extraction (i.e., entity extraction and intent recognition) from the conversation with the user.

Figure 2 shows a generic version of the storylines as depicted below.

Story #1 - Target Feature Selection

Chatbot: Hi there! I noticed you used <Strava> to <plan a route>. As a suggestion, you could <create a task> with the generated data.
Bob: Not really. What else could I do?
Chatbot: Here is a list of suggested features you could do now: <schedule an event> and <send an email>.
Bob: OK let's <schedule an event>.

Story #2 - Target App Selection

Chatbot: Would you like to <schedule an event> with <Simple Calendar>?
Bob: Which other apps can I use?
Chatbot: Here is a list of suggested apps you could use to <schedule an event>: <Google Calendar> and <MyCalendar>.
Bob: OK use <Simple Calendar>.

Story #3 - Parameter Integration

Chatbot: To <schedule an event> with <Simple Calendar>, I will use the following data:
- <event-name> as <route-name> (i.e., "Hiking Trail in Montseny")
- <location> as <start-location> (i.e., "Km 21 ctra. BV-5114 Santa Fe del, Montseny, 08470, Barcelona")
Bob: Change the event's <location> to the route's <end location> and set the <event name> to <"Lunch after hiking">

Story #4 - Custom Parameters

Chatbot: To <schedule an event> with <Simple Calendar>, I'm missing the following details:
- <start-datetime>
- <end-datetime>
- <invites>
Bob: Schedule the event on <March 26th>, starting at <1:00 p.m.> and ending at <3:00 p.m.>. Invite my usual <friend list>.

Fig. 2. Chatbot main storylines for task-oriented dialogue management

Target Feature Selection. From a source feature in the user's device (i.e., trigger for a feature integration) the chatbot queries the knowledge base for potential feature integrations based on the user's device feature. It then selects the best integration for the user by querying their preferred integration history (C3). Finally, it asks the user if they want to proceed with the integration. The user has mainly 3 options (C2): (1) to accept the feature integration proposal; (2) to deny the proposal and finish the conversation; or (3) to request new integration suggestions (as in Story #1, Fig. 2).

Target App Selection. For a given target intent, the chatbot requires a target app to enact the feature. Similarly to target feature selection, the apps suggested by the chatbot are queried from the knowledge base through the *preferred-integration* (C3) relations (updated through historic data and user feedback (C1)). Once again, the user might respond (C2): (1) to accept the application selection; (2) to refuse the selection and end the process; or (3) to request application suggestions for integration (as in Story #2, Fig. 2).

Parameter Integration. For a given feature integration, the chatbot must determine what information from the source intent can be parsed to the target intent (C4). The knowledge base contains information on which of these parameters can be reused (i.e., parameter integration). The chatbot presents the suggested parameter integrations for user validation. Overall, the user might want: (1) to accept all suggested parameter integrations; or (2) to recursively change and refactor parameter integrations with different source parameters or with custom values (as in Story #3, Fig. 2). Consequently, if desired, the user has the option to re-arrange the information in different ways.

Custom Parameters. Given that the target intent requires more data or has any optional fields the user might want to fill in, the chatbot attempts to recompile the remaining information from the user (i.e., parameters for which there is no explicit integration). For each remaining parameter, the user might want: (1) to input custom values for that specific feature integration enactment (as in Story #4, Fig. 2); or (2) to reference source intent parameters, suggesting a new potential parameter integration. Similarly to the parameter integration story, the user can recursively change the input data until final validation.

4   Component Design and NLU Pipeline

Figure 3 shows the proposed, work-in-progress machine-learning pipeline for the chatbot aiming at supporting the stories depicted in Sect. 3. The chatbot[1] is being developed using the RASA framework[2].

User Intent Pre-processing. As a first step, the pipeline processes the user intent through multiple state-of-the-art, standard NL-based components before feeding the user intent to the custom pipeline components. These include: (1) a tokenizer; (2) multiple feature extraction components (e.g., regex-based,

---

[1] Available at: https://github.com/gessi-chatbots/knowledge_based_chatbot.
[2] RASA: Open-source conversational AI framework: https://rasa.com/.

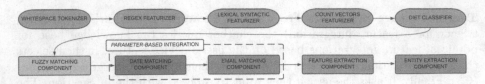

Fig. 3. Chatbot NLU Pipeline

lexical, syntactic, sentence embeddings); and (3) a Dual Intent Entity Transformer (DIET) for intent classification and entity extraction [3].

Custom NLU Pipeline. To address the specific challenges and dialogue management requirements from our design, we have extended the NLU pipeline with multiple customized, adapted components. Mainly:

- **Fuzzy matching.** Embedded the fuzzy matching technique for effective resolution of spelling mistakes and deviations from the user input [8], to avoid potential mismatches between the user intents (i.e., feature and parameter recognition) and the knowledge base modelled data.
- **Parameter-based extraction.** Prior to model-based entity extraction, we extended the pipeline with rule-based extraction techniques for standard data types (e.g., dates, e-mails) from our parameter data model (e.g., regular expressions, custom classifiers).
- **Feature extraction.** To find source and target features, we extended the pipeline with a pre-trained language model fine-tuned for feature extraction using crowdsourced data in the mobile app domain (C4). We conducted initial fine-tuning experiments with BERT [4] and T5 [12], which have shown success in abstractive summarization. The pre-trained model extracts intended features from user input. If the intent requires application features, the system can provide some from the user text.
- **Entity extraction.** We aim to enhance the pipeline by incorporating a named-entity recognition model to extract particular data types from the knowledge base parameters data model (e.g., names of individuals, organizations, phone numbers, addresses), similar to the feature extraction process (C4). For composite intents (i.e., referring to multiple parameters), we exploit the attention mechanism provided by the transformer sentence embeddings to disambiguate between multiple parameters with a shared data type (e.g., start/end date in Fig. 2).

5 Planned Evaluation

The evaluation plan is mainly structured into two sub-sets of experiments and evaluation tasks. The first one is oriented to the technical verification of the NLU pipeline and the specific components used for dialogue management, and intent and entity extraction tasks. We plan to build a validation set of annotated documents (e.g., documents, texts, user intents) which will be used for evaluating these components separately. Through a cross-validation analysis technique, this evaluation will be focused on accuracy, precision, recall, and f-measure metrics, as well as an analysis of the models' performance. Additionally, we plan to focus on the analysis of the conversation flow and the tracking of user feedback. To this end, we plan to conduct user validation studies, which will allow us to monitor and analyse user interactions with the chatbot. On one hand, we plan to focus on conversation flow analysis, to evaluate the compliance of the stories with the user's expectations. This will allow us to see deviations from default story paths or repeated errors, as well as the confidence with which our models predict intents, capture entities and identify features. On the other hand, processing user feedback will provide a general overview in terms of user satisfaction, user adherence, and learnability of the system (among others) to assess the quality degree of the stories as designed.

6   Related Work

Composite task-oriented chatbots and adaptive knowledge bases are undergoing intense study as a consequence of the latest innovations in the field of natural language. Concerning the former, Bouguelia et al. proposed a knowledge system for composite intent resolution in task-oriented chatbots [2]. While effective for the task at hand, they did not consider using user historical data processes or adaptive content techniques for the knowledge system. In this sense, Qin et al. proposed a knowledge base query by combining user intent with a given dialogue history [11], but with no specific adaptive content strategy. Xue et al. effectively applied user feedback to retrain models for a given NLU pipeline [15]. Similarly, Sapna et al. extended this model retraining task with user data from third-party software systems (i.e., external to the chatbot) [14]. Concerning adaptive knowledge bases, Raghu et al. proposed a language-resolution-based technique for knowledge base adaptations to improve user adherence [13]. Huang et al. designed a crowd-powered approach based on user feedback and focused on user stories and chatbot responses, similarly towards the same objective [5]. Overall, these studies provide a clear perspective on related work addressing a specific challenge from the design dimensions addressed in this paper.

7   Conclusions and Future Work

This paper introduces a task-oriented, knowledge-based chatbot to support the semi-automatic integration of multiple features in the context of mobile software ecosystems. Its design is oriented to illustrate the applicability of adaptive, personalized experience mechanisms and complex intent and entity resolution techniques. The following steps will require (i) the latest development stages of the machine learning pipeline components, (ii) design of the knowledge base query operations and integration of the chatbot with the knowledge base, and (iii) experimentation for verification of the custom machine learning components and validation of the conversational process with users.

Acknowledgments. With the support from the Secretariat for Universities and Research of the Ministry of Business and Knowledge of the Government of Catalonia and the European Social Fund. This paper has been funded by the Spanish Ministerio de Ciencia e Innovación under project/funding scheme PID2020-117191RB-I00/AEI/10.13039/501100011033.

References

1. Bavaresco, R., et al.: Conversational agents in business: a systematic literature review and future research directions. Comput. Sci. Rev. **36**, 100239 (2020)
2. Bouguelia, S., Brabra, H., Benatallah, B., Baez, M., Zamanirad, S., Kheddouci, H.: Context knowledge-aware recognition of composite intents in task-oriented human-bot conversations. In: Franch, X., Poels, G., Gailly, F., Snoeck, M. (eds.) CAiSE 2022. LNCS, vol. 13295, pp. 237–252. Springer, Cham (2022). https://doi.org/10.1007/978-3-031-07472-1_14
3. Bunk, T., et al.: DIET: lightweight language understanding for dialogue systems (2020). https://doi.org/10.48550/ARXIV.2004.09936
4. Devlin, J., et al.: BERT: pre-training of deep bidirectional transformers for language understanding (2018). https://doi.org/10.48550/ARXIV.1810.04805
5. Huang, T., Chang, J., Bigham, J.: Evorus: a crowd-powered conversational assistant built to automate itself over time. In: Proceedings of the 2018 CHI Conference on Human Factors in Computing Systems (2018)
6. Hussain, S., Ameri Sianaki, O., Ababneh, N.: A survey on conversational agents/chatbots classification and design techniques. In: Barolli, L., Takizawa, M., Xhafa, F., Enokido, T. (eds.) WAINA 2019. AISC, vol. 927, pp. 946–956. Springer, Cham (2019). https://doi.org/10.1007/978-3-030-15035-8_93
7. Jain, M., et al.: Evaluating and informing the design of chatbots. In: Proceedings of the 2018 Designing Interactive Systems Conference, pp. 895–906 (2018)
8. Kalyanathaya, K., Akila, D., Suseendran, G.: A fuzzy approach to approximate string matching for text retrieval in NLP. J. Comput. Inf. Syst. **15**, 26–32 (2019)
9. Motger, Q., Franch, X., Marco, J.: Integrating adaptive mechanisms into mobile applications exploiting user feedback. In: Cherfi, S., Perini, A., Nurcan, S. (eds.) RCIS 2021. LNBIP, vol. 415, pp. 347–355. Springer, Cham (2021). https://doi.org/10.1007/978-3-030-75018-3_23
10. Motger, Q., Franch, X., Marco, J.: Software-based dialogue systems: survey, taxonomy, and challenges. ACM Comput. Surv. **55**(5), 1–42 (2022)
11. Qin, L., et al.: Entity-consistent end-to-end task-oriented dialogue system with KB retriever. In: EMNLP-IJCNLP 2019, pp. 133–142 (2019)
12. Raffel, C., et al.: Exploring the limits of transfer learning with a unified text-to-text transformer (2019). https://doi.org/10.48550/ARXIV.1910.10683
13. Raghu, D., Gupta, N., Mausam: Disentangling language and knowledge in task-oriented dialogs. In: NAACL HLT 2019, vol. 1, pp. 1239–1255 (2019)
14. Sapna, et al.: Recommendence and fashionsence: online fashion advisor for offline experience. In: CoDS-COMAD 2019 (2019)
15. Xue, Z., et al.: Isa: intuit smart agent, a neural-based agent-assist chatbot. In: 2018 IEEE International Conference on Data Mining Workshops (ICDMW) (2018)

Cicero: An AI-Based Writing Assistant for Legal Users

Francesca De Luzi(✉) , Mattia Macrì, Massimo Mecella ,
and Tommaso Mencattini

Sapienza Università di Roma, Rome, Italy
{francesca,mattia,massimo,tommaso}@diag.uniroma1.it

Abstract. This paper presents the problem statement and the research approach on an Italian project in the field of e-justice. We present the motivation and methodology for the application of an automatic writing assistant pipeline to Italian civil cases. The proposed solution is based on fine-tuning a transformer on a pre-processed corpus of Italian civil judgments. The resulting language model may be deployed as a writing assistant for legal users, in order to improve the efficiency of text writing, or further fine-tuned to be deployed in other law-related NLP tasks.

Keywords: e-justice · legal text generation · language models

1 Introduction

In this paper, a writing assistant for legal text is introduced in the context of e-government, which is a field of applied informatics focusing on improving the efficiency and transparency of government operations [14]. In particular, this paper originates from the e-justice Giustizia Agile project, an initiative promoted by the Italian Ministry of Justice aimed at improving: *(i)* the efficiency and performance of judicial offices through technological innovation, *(ii)* the organizational support for computerization and telematization of judicial offices and *(iii)* the activation of change management operations.

Starting from a mapping of the operational processes of the judicial offices and a surveying of the organization and functioning of the Process Offices (UpP)[1] and of the information systems in use, we tried to locate the critical issues that most impact judicial processes as a whole. The various interviews have shown that some activities more than others have a strong impact on the two main KPIs of interest: *(i) Disposition Time* (DT), to measure the length of administrative procedures in the courts and to estimate the impact of delays in terms of the costs of the procedures; *(ii)* the *Clearance Rate* (CR), defined as the relationship between the processes judged and the new cases coming. Indeed, Italy has been

---

[1] In the recent Italian reform of the Italian judicial offices, a new function was created, named "Ufficio per il Processo" (in Italian, in English it might be "Office for the Judicial Process").

C. Cabanillas and F. Perez (Eds.): CAiSE 2023, LNBIP 477, pp. 103–111, 2023.
https://doi.org/10.1007/978-3-031-34674-3_13

classified in 2018 as one of the worst European countries concerning the efficiency of civil and criminal proceedings by the European Commission for the Efficiency of Justice [4]. Furthermore, the reduction of the disposition time of civil and criminal proceedings has been pointed out as one of the objectives of Italy's recovery and resilience plan[2].

Among the activities mentioned above, the long process of writing legal documents (judgments) and the continuous production of summaries for the judge were the most emphasized by the interviewed users. Addressing these needs requires new tools to improve the quality of court decisions and speed up procedures and actions. This approach would not only save time but also improve the uniformity and quality of written output. To structure our analysis properly, make design decisions explicit and motivate the need for the proposed solutions we were inspired by [8]. Based on these considerations, we formulated the following research question:

Can a writing assistant help the Italian justice system?

To address the aforementioned research question, this paper introduces Cicero[3], a legal writing assistant, whose aim is to improve the efficiency of trials by assisting judges in judgments' drafting. Moreover, the usage of Cicero could also be extended to new employees in the UpP role by automatically generating parts of the text of the judgments. To train a preliminary version of Cicero only a subset of the currently available documents has been deployed; that is, the model has been fine-tuned on about twenty thousand civil judgments out of the one million judgments provided directly by the Italian Ministry of Justice.

The rest of the paper is organized as follows. After a discussion of the related work in Sect. 2, in Sect. 3 we describe the proposed approach for automatic legal writing. In Sects. 4 and 5 we address the usability of this artifact and our plan to evaluate it. Finally, Sect. 6 is devoted to ongoing and future work.

2   Related Work

In recent years, the effectiveness of Natural Language Processing pipelines has constantly improved thanks to the successful introduction of transformer models [12]. In particular, language modeling techniques have achieved surprising and constantly evolving results thanks to the usage of the foregoing architecture [20]. Nowadays, large pre-trained language models are capable of delivering state-of-the-art performance on a broad range of downstream tasks by leveraging semantically-rich embeddings and deep contextual understanding [20]; in particular, they relevantly improved the quality of the text generated by novel Natural Language Generation (NLG) pipelines [20]. In particular, the so-called *writing assistants* received a huge boost from recent advances of language models [5].

---

[2] https://commission.europa.eu/business-economy-euro/economic-recovery/recovery-and-resilience-facility/italys-recovery-and-resilience-plan_en.

[3] Cicero, the well-known politician and writer in the ancient Rome, was also a lawyer appreciated for his eloquence.

One of the first models to apply the transformer architecture to the task of language modeling and achieved state-of-the-art results on several NLP benchmarks was BERT (Bidirectional Encoder Representations from Transformers); thereafter, a series of subsequent models enhanced LLM performance in various activities. These include Transformer-XL, RoBERTa, ELECTRA, ALBERT (A Lite BERT), T5 (Text-to-Text Transformer), PEGASUS, and the GPT (Generative Pre-trained Transformer) model series [9]. The legal domain is taking the challenge posed by these models, which are still poorly experimented. These include *LegalBERT* [3], which was built by pre-training BERT model on several legal corpora; *LamBERTa* [18] is also built on an Italian BERT model that was pre-trained using the Italian Civil Code and used for the articles retrieval; *ALeaseBERT* [11] which was pre-trained and fine-tuned on lease data. Despite the importance of BERT, in our work, we focused and deployed on GPT-2, [16], owing to the generative nature of writing assistants' tasks. GPT2 is also a transformer-based language model that uses self-attention mechanisms to model the dependencies between words in a text sequence. It is trained using a generative language modeling objective, where the model is tasked with predicting the next word in a sequence given the previous context [16].

In spite of the improved performances, practical application of the aforementioned large language models should take into account both the technical challenges derived from requiring significant computing power due to the large amount of data they are trained on and the scale of these models. Furthermore, another challenge derives from the scarcity of multilingual language models, especially if compared to English ones. In order to tackle these shortcomings and allow models to efficiently learn from specific legal Italian datasets, balanced-scale language model for Italian should be deployed [6], just as our approach provides. With regards to further applications of artificial intelligence in e-government, there have been several commendable examples in Europe, such as the use of AI for quick reading, classification, and attribution of documents to the chancellor's office, tested in Austria[4]; or the use of chatbots to steer the citizen towards an alternative dispute resolution, as in Latvia[5]; or the *Claudette* [13] system in France to identify unfair terms in contracts and information. In the national landscape, we can mention the *Toga*[6] system, dedicated exclusively to the criminal lawyer and that allows you to obtain operational information on each crime, calculate the terms and deadlines, and manage the events of each procedure; or writing systems, drafting legal acts and standard phrases such as *Ulysses*[7] and *Textexpander*[8].

---

[4] https://rm.coe.int/how-is-austria-approaching-ai-integration-into-judicial-policies-/16808e4d81.

[5] https://reform-support.ec.europa.eu/what-we-do/public-administration-and-governance/development-latvian-judicial-system_en.

[6] https://toga.cloud/.

[7] https://ulysses.app/.

[8] https://textexpander.com/.

3   Methodology

In this section, we present our methodology for generating coherent Italian text using a multi-stage pipeline. The pipeline (see Fig. 1) takes in input a set of Italian judgments, which undergo a pre-processing phase to extract and clean relevant data. We then discuss the fine-tuning phase of a GPT-2 language model, where the model learns to recognize patterns in the input data to improve text generation and optimize performance minimizing perplexity scores.

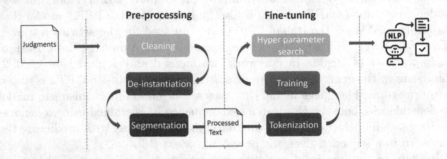

Fig. 1. Pipeline.

3.1   Pre-processing

In the pre-processing phase, the initial documents are refined to be ready for building the required dataset for fine-tuning the model [1]. The pre-processing of civil judgments requires overcoming a challenge derived several challenges derived from specific features of these documents. Among them, the most critical challenge regards the juridical vocabulary, related to the legal lexicon and uncommon in ordinary Italian. In particular, the pre-processing was divided into three steps: cleaning the document, de-instantiation of its named entities, and segmentation of the documents into smaller data points.

Firstly, data cleaning involves removing any irrelevant information from the textual data. This helps to reduce the noise in the data. With regards to text generation, data cleaning must not impact relevantly the actual text. Indeed, the final aim of text generation is to return a new text sample that replicates the original style of the text. Therefore, extensive data cleaning may eliminate important details that should have been learned. For this reason, we limited the data cleaning phase to solely remove those words or markers that are associated with the structure of the judgments (such as signatures or abbreviations), to gather the plain text that would have been used for the model. Indeed, while the model must learn the style of the legal lingo, it is not required to learn the structure of the judgments.

Secondly, the document was de-instantiated. This is a novel data pre-processing technique that was added to our pipeline, based on NER[9]. The idea

---

[9] Actually, one could interpret de-instantiation as a type of masking [2], where, rather than using an anonymous mask, a semi-anonymous NER token is deployed.

was to pre-process the text in such a way that named entities, such as people, locations, and laws would have been substituted with the name of their classes [7]. In such a way, the language model would learn to return those special tokens during the next generation, rather than a particular law, proper name, or location. The main factor behind this design choice is derived from the role of the model once in production: a writing assistant for legal users. Indeed, the model should generate general sentences that can be instantiated by the legal user with the particular details of his/her case. In practice, a pre-trained NER model from Spacy[10] was used to label the entities in the text. Once the entities were labeled, they have been substituted with a special token based on their labels (such as LAW). The Spacy model was already fine-tuned on the legal domain and downloaded from Hugging Face[11]. Figure 2 shows an example of de-instantiation, where references to names, locations, dates, and other informations are fictitious.

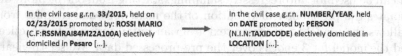

Fig. 2. De-instantiated sentence from a legal judgment (already translated).

Lastly, the documents have been segmented into smaller chunks. This is required for two reasons. Firstly, it allowed us to eliminate useless details regarding the structure and the division of the judgment. Secondly, reducing the dimension of the documents was required due to the polynomial scalability of the memory of Large Language Models over the input size. The first step of this phase was to divide the judgment into chapters. Indeed, some of the chapters of a judgment do not contain any useful information for the model but they just present some formal information about the judges, the tribunal, and the parts of the process. Once we extracted the searched chapters, we segmented them into sentences through a Spacy Model. Thereafter, a new corpus of smaller sentences was built and the initial corpus of judgments was discarded.

3.2   Fine-Tuning

The fine-tuning phase consists of several steps, including tokenization, model training, and hyperparameter search. The starting point was to select the language model that had to be fine-tuned. Based on language and hardware constraints, a small Italian language model with 124M parameters has been chosen. In particular, it is a model with a GPT-2 architecture [16].

Specifically, the language model was already adapted to Italian through a novel technique based on retraining lexical embeddings to gain embeddings for

---

[10] https://spacy.io.
[11] https://huggingface.co/bullmount/it_nerIta_trf.

Italian that are aligned with GPT2's original lexical embeddings [19] and that allows the model to successfully process Italian documents. Therefore, the starting point was the "GroNLP/gpt2-small-italian" checkpoint downloaded through Hugging Face[12].

The first step in fine-tuning the model was tokenization. This involves breaking down the raw text data into smaller units, known as tokens, which can be fed into the model. Tokenization is critical for creating a numerical representation of the text data that can be understood by the model. After tokenization, the model is trained using the tokenized data. During training, the model learns to recognize patterns in the input data and make accurate predictions based on those patterns [15]. The goal of training is to optimize the model's parameters in such a way that the likelihood of the training data is maximized, without reaching overfitting. Indeed, the language model should learn to estimate the probability of a word, given the previous words. Once a probabilistic model is trained, the model can be used for autoregressive sampling: starting from one or more words, it estimates the probability distribution of the next word and samples from it. This allows the model to generate text from an initial prompt. In practice, we trained the model for 3 epochs over the pre-processed data. We set the learning rate to $2e-5$ and the weight decay to 0.01, which are common hyperparameters used in training language models. The learning rate controls the step size of the gradient descent optimizer during training, while the weight decay helps to prevent overfitting by regularizing the weights of the model. The batch size was set to 2. This value was chosen based on the available memory resources on our hardware. To mitigate the effects of small batch size on training stability, we implemented gradient accumulation and checkpointing. Gradient accumulation involves accumulating the gradients of multiple small batches before updating the weights of the model, effectively simulating a larger batch size. Checkpointing involves periodically saving the state of the model during training to reduce memory usage and prevent out-of-memory errors.

Once the model has been trained, the final step is hyperparameter search. Hyperparameters are settings that determine how the model behaves during training and prediction. Examples of hyperparameters include learning rate, batch size, and the number of epochs. Even though we still did not reach this point, we plan to carry out an initial random search, that will be followed up by a trial-and-error approach, based on the insights derived from the random search. In practice, we will pick the hyperparameters that minimize the perplexity of the model. The perplexity of a model is a commonly used metric for evaluating the quality of a language model that measures how well the language model can predict the next word in a sequence of text. A lower perplexity score indicates that the model is better at predicting the next word, and therefore has a better understanding of the underlying language.

---

[12] https://huggingface.co/GroNLP/gpt2-small-italian.

4   Usability

As established by art. 132[13]. of the Italian Code of Civil Procedure, a fundamental step in each civil lawsuit is the drafting of the judgment for its subsequent filing and publication. Therefore, we aim to optimize the overall DT and CR of the civil procedure by improving the efficiency of the drafting phase through the usage of Cicero. In particular, Cicero assists the writing process by suggesting n possible masked completion of the current sentence. Furthermore, the generation of a de-instantiated sentence allows for minimizing the time unproductively spent in correcting the hallucination of the language model (see Fig. 3). Furthermore, the usability of Cicero is not limited to judges. Firstly, the model can be used by any legal user, as it will be made available on Hugging Face Hub[14] and can be run with a single 12 GB GPU. Moreover, Cicero can be a valuable resource for Italian NLP practitioners given the scarcity of pre-trained models for Italian text generation [17], and the absence of an Italian generative language model explicitly fine-tuned for legal lexicon.

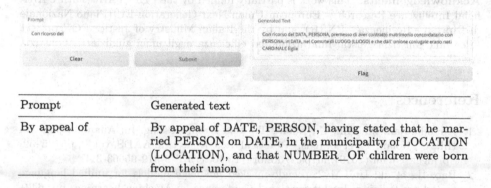

Prompt	Generated text
By appeal of	By appeal of DATE, PERSON, having stated that he married PERSON on DATE, in the municipality of LOCATION (LOCATION), and that NUMBER_OF children were born from their union

Fig. 3. Example of text generated from an input prompt and its translation.

5   Evaluation

To carry out the evaluation we follow the recommendations and best practices as suggested by [10]. The goal is to evaluate (both with humans and using automated metrics) the output quality of Cicero, so we take an intrinsic approach using a questionnaire to get feedback from participants, with a focus on properties of text along with some metrics such as the perplexity. Our plan is to test Cicero in the context of a specific use case: comparing sentences extracted from a real judgment to those automatically generated by different tools (Cicero, ChatGPT[15], and GePpeTto [6]). To do this we design a series of surveys in

---

[13] https://www.gazzettaufficiale.it/sommario/codici/proceduraCivile.

[14] https://huggingface.co/docs/hub/index.

[15] ChatGPT is an AI-based chatbot model developed by OpenAI that specializes in conversations with a human user.

which Cicero is compared with other extracts to measure the user's ability to distinguish legal extracts generated by Cicero from others.

6 Ongoing and Future Work

In this work, we presented a preliminary pipeline for the automatic writing of sentences of the judgment of a judicial process that uses the instructions and capabilities of a language model. The project is ongoing and the work will be further developed and expanded. To enhance our approach, it will be essential to maintain ongoing collaboration with professionals and specialists in related fields, such as law. The interviews carried out so far have proved very useful in uncovering new research directions and understanding the specificity of legal documents through the promising technology of legal language models [15]. In future work, finding well-performing models for each step of the pipeline and evaluating the conduct of such models is our next immediate steps.

Acknowledgements. This work is partially funded by the PE1 - FAIR (Future Artificial Intelligence Research) - European Union Next-Generation-EU (Piano Nazionale di Ripresa e Resilienza - PNRR), and by the Italian Ministry of Justice PON project "Per una Giustizia giusta: Innovazione ed efficienza negli uffici giudiziari - Giustizia Agile".

References

1. Anandarajan, M., Hill, C., Nolan, T.: Text Preprocessing. In: Anandarajan, M., Hill, C., Nolan, T., et al. (eds.) Practical Text Analytics. AADS, vol. 2, pp. 45–59. Springer, Cham (2019). https://doi.org/10.1007/978-3-319-95663-3_4
2. Bao, H., et al.: UniLMv2: pseudo-masked language models for unified language model pre-training. In: International Conference on Machine Learning, pp. 642–652. PMLR (2020)
3. Chalkidis, I., Fergadiotis, M., Malakasiotis, P., Aletras, N., Androutsopoulos, I.: LEGAL-BERT: the muppets straight out of law school. arXiv preprint arXiv:2010.02559 (2020)
4. Council of Europe: European judicial systems: efficiency and quality of justice. CEPEJ Stud. **26**, 1–338 (2018)
5. Dale, R., Viethen, J.: The automated writing assistance landscape in 2021. Nat. Lang. Eng. **27**(4), 511–518 (2021)
6. De Mattei, L., Cafagna, M., Dell'Orletta, F., Nissim, M., Guerini, M.: GePpeTto carves Italian into a language model. In: 7th Italian Conference on Computational Linguistics, CLiC-it 2020 (2020)
7. Di Martino, B., Marulli, F., Lupi, P., Cataldi, A.: A machine learning based methodology for automatic annotation and anonymisation of privacy-related items in textual documents for justice domain. In: Barolli, L., Poniszewska-Maranda, A., Enokido, T. (eds.) CISIS 2020. AISC, vol. 1194, pp. 530–539. Springer, Cham (2021). https://doi.org/10.1007/978-3-030-50454-0_55
8. Johannesson, P., Perjons, E.: An Introduction to Design Science. Springer, Cham (2014). https://doi.org/10.1007/978-3-319-10632-8

9. Kalyan, K.S., Rajasekharan, A., Sangeetha, S.: AMMUS: a survey of transformer-based pretrained models in natural language processing. arXiv preprint arXiv:2108.05542 (2021)

10. van der Lee, C., Gatt, A., van Miltenburg, E., Krahmer, E.: Human evaluation of automatically generated text: current trends and best practice guidelines. Comput. Speech Lang. **67**, 101151 (2021)

11. Leivaditi, S., Rossi, J., Kanoulas, E.: A benchmark for lease contract review. arXiv preprint arXiv:2010.10386 (2020)

12. Lin, T., Wang, Y., Liu, X., Qiu, X.: A survey of transformers. AI Open **3**, 111–132 (2022)

13. Lippi, M., et al.: CLAUDETTE: an automated detector of potentially unfair clauses in online terms of service. Artif. Intell. Law **27**(2), 117–139 (2019). https://doi.org/10.1007/s10506-019-09243-2

14. Mahajan, N.: E-governance: its role, importance and challenges. Int. J. Curr. Innov. Res. **1**(10), 237–243 (2015)

15. Peric, L., Mijic, S., Stammbach, D., Ash, E.: Legal language modeling with transformers. In: 4th Workshop on Automated Semantic Analysis of Information in Legal Text (ASAIL 2020), vol. 2764. CEUR-WS (2020)

16. Radford, A., Wu, J., Child, R., Luan, D., Amodei, D., Sutskever, I., et al.: Language models are unsupervised multitask learners. OpenAI Blog **1**(8), 9 (2019)

17. Sarti, G., Nissim, M.: IT5: large-scale text-to-text pretraining for Italian language understanding and generation (2022)

18. Tagarelli, A., Simeri, A.: Unsupervised law article mining based on deep pre-trained language representation models with application to the Italian civil code. Artif. Intell. Law **30**, 417–473 (2022). https://doi.org/10.1007/s10506-021-09301-8

19. de Vries, W., Nissim, M.: As good as new. How to successfully recycle English GPT-2 to make models for other languages. arXiv preprint arXiv:2012.05628 (2020)

20. Zhao, W.X., et al.: A survey of large language models. arXiv preprint arXiv:2303.18223 (2023)

AIDA: A Tool for Resiliency in Smart Manufacturing

Giuseppe De Giacomo[1,2], Marco Favorito[3], Francesco Leotta[1],
Massimo Mecella[1], Flavia Monti[1(✉)], and Luciana Silo[1]

[1] Sapienza Università di Roma, Rome, Italy
{degiacomo,leotta,mecella,monti,silo}@diag.uniroma1.it
[2] University of Oxford, Oxford, UK
[3] Banca d'Italia, Rome, Italy
marco.favorito@bancaditalia.it

Abstract. One of the salient features of Industry 4.0 is that machines
and other actors involved in the manufacturing process provide Industrial APIs that allow to inquire their status. In order to provide resilience,
the manufacturing process should be able to automatically adapt to new
conditions, considering new actors for the fulfillment of the manufacturing goals. As a single manufacturing process may include several of
these actors, and their interfaces are often complex, this task cannot be
easily accomplished in a completely manual way. In this work, we focus
on the orchestration of Industrial APIs using Markov Decision Processes
(MDPs). We present a tool implementing stochastic composition of processes and we demonstrate it in an Industry 4.0 scenario.

Keywords: industrial API · smart manufacturing · service
composition

1 Introduction

The term Industry 4.0 refers to the emergence and diffusion of new technologies which allow the development of fully automatized production processes [16].
Smart manufacturing is nowadays a term highly used in conjunction with the
concept of Industry 4.0; it aims at improving the manufacturing processes in
order to increase productivity and quality, make workers' lives easier, and define
new business opportunities. This is enabled by leveraging on innovative techniques like Artificial Intelligence (AI), big data analytics and Process Mining
(PM). The adoption of such techniques enables the advent of AI-augmented
Business Process Management Systems (ABPMSs), an emerging class of process-
aware information systems [9]. Such a trend has made it possible to create new
opportunities for interoperability, modularity, distributed processing, and integration in real-time with other systems for industrial processes.

One of the main characteristics of Industry 4.0 is that actors involved in the
manufacturing process (e.g., machines, humans) provide Application Program-

---

M. Favorito—The author's views are his own, and they do not reflect those of his
employer.

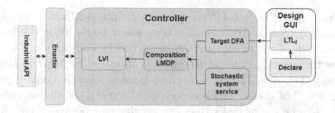

Fig. 1. Architecture of AIDA tool

ming Interfaces (APIs) which allow to collect their status [4] and to operate on them. The term status here does not only encompass the current situation of the actor, but also information resulting from the application of diagnostic, predictive and prescriptive analytics models. A single manufacturing process may include tens of different actors along the supply chain [2] which may suddenly fail or provides bad performance. At any moment, in order to provide resilience, a manufacturing process should be able to automatically adapt to new conditions, considering new actors for the fulfillment of the manufacturing goals. This task cannot be done manually when actors span multiple organizations possibly separated from both the geographical and organizational points of view.

In this paper, we propose a tool that generates a plan for a manufacturing process. Manufacturing actors are depicted as services (Industrial APIs) that reflect their behaviors. Particularly, we employ the generalization of the service composition approach in a stochastic setting [3], in which the services have an unpredictable behavior and are subject to wear. In our tool, instead of representing the manufacturing process as a target stochastic service, we use the well-known formalism DECLARE, widely used in the Business Process Management literature. Another important contribution that we provide is to achieve an optimal solution for the orchestration by solving a probabilistic planning problem formalized as Lexicographic Markov Decision Process (LMDP), which permits to take into account not only the breaking probability of a machine but also a scenario of multiple objectives. In this way, we are able to *autonomously* obtain a production planning which is *adaptive*, as it changes every time that the manufacturing of a new product or batch is started, and *context-aware*, as it depends on the current status of involved actors. Our tool is implemented in a software prototype, which will be showcased in a scenario concerning an electric motor manufacturing process derived from a real industrial project.

2 Tool Architecture

Figure 1 depicts the architecture of our tool AIDA - Adaptive InDustrial APIs[1].

We implement a *service-oriented* approach for industrial manufacturing to enable the interoperability between the actors. Particularly, we model each actor involved in the manufacturing process as a service, thus creating a service-based supply chain consisting of a composition of services (representing actors). Such

---

[1] Aida is also the name of a famous opera by Verdi, somehow inspired by the making of Suez Canal: undoubtedly an example of smart manufacturing for the time being.

services realized as *Industrial APIs*, represent the physical actors describing their functionalities (or tasks). Additionally, they allow to monitor the behavior and status information of the actors and allow to invoke commands.

We define the actors as *stochastic services* modeled as *Markov Decision Processes (MDPs)* [17]. An MDP is a discrete-time stochastic control process containing *(i)* a set Σ of states which represent the status of the service, *(ii)* a set A of actions i.e., the set of tasks that the service can perform, *(iii)* a transition function P that returns for every state s and action a a distribution over the next state i.e., the probability of the service to end in a certain status performing a certain task, *(iv)* a reward function R that specifies the reward when transitioning from state s to state s' by executing action a, and *(v)* a discount factor $\lambda \in (0,1)$ which determines how important future rewards are to the current state. If $\lambda = 0$, the service is "myopic" in being concerned only with maximizing immediate rewards. As λ reaches 1, the method becomes more "farsighted", more strongly considering future rewards.

Particularly we are interested in LMDPs (Lexicographic MDP) [22] in which the reward function is a vector of reward functions. This vector is formed by two objectives: the cost and the quality of the product; and our goal is to minimize the former and maximize the latter. An optimal solution to an LMDP is a policy ρ^* which assigns an action to each state and maximizes the expected cumulative reward, i.e., the sum of discounted rewards when starting at state s and choosing actions based on ρ following a lexicographic preference.

We describe the behavior of each actor as a state machine with a probabilistic behavior represented as an MDP and maintained by the corresponding Industrial API. The latter contains the set of transitions (states, actions, probabilities and costs) that an actor is able to perform and the information relative to the initial, final and current state. Each actor may include a rich set of states (i.e., READY, CONFIGURATION, EXECUTING, BROKEN, REPAIRING) and actions or only a subset. Different actors can offer the same operation. As a consequence, an actor chosen for a specific process instance could be discarded for the later instance. The Industrial APIs expose endpoints to retrieve their information which are combined to construct a community of stochastic services, i.e., a *stochastic system service*. Intuitively, the stochastic system service status includes the current status of all the composing services, and a specific action performed on the system service changes only one component of the current state, corresponding to the service selected to execute that action.

Among others, we define the manufacturing process specification as DECLARE constraints, i.e., LTL$_f$ formula φ [8] over the set of propositions $\mathcal{P}$ that specifies the allowed traces of the process. We allow the potential production process engineer to specify the process (in a canvas as in Fig. 2) via the *design GUI*. Note that the collection of services representing the actors can perform actions in $\mathcal{P}$ and, moreover, to make our model richer we allow services to execute a broader set of actions. Moreover, we put each LTL$_f$ formula in conjunction in order to compute the equivalent deterministic finite automaton (DFA) (made by Lydia tool [6]), i.e., *target DFA*.

Given both the stochastic system service and the target DFA, we compute the *composition LMDP* as a function that contains: all the states of the target DFA and the stochastic system service, all the actions of the services, the probability of ending in a certain system state performing an action, and the vector of reward functions formed by the objectives that we want to consider in our application. In practice, it consists of a cartesian product operation of both the system and target services. According to a specific target (manufacturing goal), it computes all the possible executions of the manufacturing process, i.e., by combining together the specifications of all the actors (stochastic services) and the goal, it identifies all the possible status of the actors at any step.

We extract the optimal policy of the composition LMDP by executing the *Lexicographic Value Iteration (LVI)* Algorithm [22]. Such a policy contains the specification of the optimal actions (and related services) to execute from each possible state in order to reach the final goal.

The *enactor* acts as a middleware that interfaces with the Industrial APIs in order to check whether the current status and the transition functions have changed (for instance because of the wearing out during the execution). We distinguish two different resilience scenarios. On the one hand, when only the status of an actor changes, the *controller* is able to choose the next action to be performed by checking the result of the optimal policy from the new state formed. On the other hand, when both the status and the transition function of an actor change, the *controller* re-computes the optimal policy from an up-to-date composition LMDP which includes the latest condition of the service. Through the Industrial APIs, the *enactor* calls the services identified in the optimal policy computed by the *controller*.

3   Demonstrating the AIDA Tool

A freely available tool[2] has been implemented. The tool can be configured to prioritize either cost or quality. This is particularly helpful in a real industrial context, as a company may prefer to reduce costs (e.g., for timing or pecuniary reasons) or, on the contrary, to maximize quality. Noticeably, the decision of the priority can be possibly seen as a customer decision in the case of so called mass-customization.

To demonstrate the proposed tool, we use the manufacturing process of an electric motor which is depicted in Fig. 2 using the DECLARE formalism [15]. For the sake of brevity, we focus on the main aspects of the process, but the formalization can be easily extended to cover the process much more in detail.

The main components of an electric motor are the stator, the rotor and, in the case of alternate current motors with direct current power, an inverter. These three components are built or retrieved in any order and then eventually assembled to build a motor (*alternate succession* constraint). After the motor is assembled, a Running In test must be performed (*alternate succession* constraint), and, optionally (*alternate precedence* constraint), at most one

---

[2] See sources at https://github.com/luusi/AIDA.

(*not coexistence* constraint) between an Electric Test and a full Static Test (the latter comprises the former). In addition, optionally (*alternate precedence* constraint), the motor can be painted. The process depicts the manufacturing tasks involved in a production of a *single motor*.

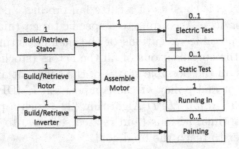

Fig. 2. The electric motor manufacturing process represented using DECLARE.

We want to find a plan that fulfills the manufacturing process, selecting appropriate actors for the actions considering the cost and quality impact of choices.

The repository contains a Python script that reproduces the case study. The script shows how the goal is achieved also in case of malfunctioning and/or exceptions raised by the Industrial APIs. For each of the services we have several instances, each showing a specific wear and reward vector. In the following, we will describe a possible execution obtained by manually choosing the values of wear and reward vectors. In a real application scenario, choices are made accordingly to the real conditions as reported by each actor digital twin.

The example manufacturing process specification allows the three *Build/Retrieve* actions to be executed in any order. As an example, the first *Build Retrieve Stator* action may be executed first, and the tool may decide to choose STATOR BUILDER service to execute the action in case the warehouse machine is more costly.

Particularly interesting is the case when an actor shows a significantly high wear. For example, the execution of the *Build Retrieve Rotor* action, can be performed, in the proposed demo, by two different machines ROTOR BUILDER 1 and ROTOR BUILDER 2, or by the ROTOR WAREHOUSE service. If the first two machines have a higher probability to end in a BROKEN state, the optimal policy will prefer the ROTOR WAREHOUSE SERVICE, because it has no possibility to break. Since the *Build Retrieve Inverter* can be performed only by the INVERTER WAREHOUSE service, in this case the choice of the tool is immediate.

At this point, the *Assemble Motor* action can be performed. Here, the controller may prefer to use the ASSEMBLER MACHINE 1 instead of using the ASSEMBLER MACHINE 2, even if they have the same cost, if the first machine has a higher quality reward.

Concerning the *Painting* action, we suppose it is offered by a machine and by a human, and we may assume that the human is more economic but gives a lower quality compared to a machine. In this case, the controller would prefer using PAINTER HUMAN service because it has a lower economic cost than the PAINTER MACHINE. Finally, for the *Smart Tester* action, the controller may prefer to use SMART TESTER 2 if it has a lower economic cost than SMART TESTER 1.

Noticeably, we have defined a tool that computes not only the right action according to several constraints but is also very resilient. Suppose that some machines end in the BROKEN state; the controller may decide to restore, for example, the STATOR BUILDER SERVICE rather than directly using the STATOR WAREHOUSE which could perform the same action at a much higher cost.

4 Related Works

The tool that we implement proposes a plan for smart manufacturing that is *resilient*. Resilience concerns the ability of a system to cope with unplanned situations in order to keep carrying out its mission. The research on resilient systems is extensively studied [23,24] mainly at a conceptual level, and continuously improved especially at design time [13]. In AIDA, we ensure resilience at run time as, when a service during its job breaks down and/or starts to have a high cost and a low quality level, we take into account all these aspects and the controller is able to adapt the plan avoiding possible not convenient services. The composition is possible thanks to the use of the Industrial APIs representing the manufacturing actors which provide lots of features like accessing the selected services [12], enabling quick integration [10] and monitoring their behaviour [19].

The implemented approach is influenced by previous works on automated service composition. Authors in [3], for example, propose a solution for the service composition in stochastic settings, defining the non-deterministic behavior of the target service. The authors though do not capture the non-deterministic behaviors of the available services, and do not take into account the rewards of using a certain service.

The problem we addressed also belongs to the area of decision-theoretic planning applied to manufacturing. Such a topic is part of the greater problem of AI planning. Different approaches are employed in planning problems, i.e., classical planning, dealing with deterministic contexts, and decision-theoretic planning, facing with non-deterministic and stochastic scenarios. Multiple works can be found in the literature employing classical planning techniques [14,21], however they do not take into account the stochasticity of manufacturing. The literature presents limited research on the application of MDPs in the manufacturing domain. Authors in [11] propose an MDP-based self-adaptive Automated Guided Vehicles (AGVs) control model that avoids collisions efficiently. The work [5] presents a hierarchical MDP approach for adaptive multi-scale prognostics and health management, maximizing the expected gain. Authors in [1] use an MDP for finding an optimal cost-effective maintenance decision based on the condition revealed at the time of inspection on a single diesel engine.

The proposed tool represents an evolution of what presented in [7]. In the original work though, the target process is represented using a state machine,

118   G. De Giacomo et al.

thus not allowing for the flexibility which is typical of certain manufacturing processes. In addition, the modeling formalism does not allow for multiple objectives. The paper represents a useful reference anyway to deepen some of the concepts behing the AIDA tool.

Another important aspect in manufacturing environments is the maintenance efficiency, where asset maintenance and repair significantly contribute to operation and support costs. In real systems, maintenance is complicated making it necessary to use many optimization criteria. The majority of research works do not adopt a data-driven approach to decision-making, and thus they are limited to specific problems and domains [18,20]. That is why mathematical optimization and rule-based systems are the most common categories of methods.

5 Concluding Remarks

In this work, we proposed a tool implementing a stochastic service composition approach with LTL$_f$ goals, where composing services have a stochastic behavior and are modeled as MDPs. The goal is to obtain an optimal policy with respect to a set of reward measures expressed as a vector with priorities. In particular, we have realized a demo showing how such a tool can be helpful in an industrial manufacturing context where DECLARE models a manufacturing process, while the availability of Industrial APIs enables the collection of information of the involved actors. Especially, rewards and probabilities associated with each service can be continuously updated by applying, for instance, predictive maintenance algorithms to monitor the status of the different involved actors, thus allowing at *each repetition of the process* to choose the most suitable actors to perform actions. This makes the process resilient to failures and optimal with respect to defined reward measures. In our demo tool, we adopt a simulator mimicking the evolution of the single actors (services) from the point of view of rewards and failure probabilities, showing how changes influence proposed execution traces. This paper impacts anyway application scenarios other than Industry 4.0, being applicable in any context where actors can be modeled as services. Finally, in this paper, we do not consider data; adding data introduces new challenges, as specific traces of the process, legal from the point of view of the control flow, might be not doable in practice. Future works include considering conditions expressed on service or process data.

Acknowledgements. This work is partially funded by the ERC project WhiteMech (no. 834228), the PRIN project RIPER (no. 20203FFYLK), the Electrospindle 4.0 project (funded by MISE, Italy, no. F/160038/01-04/X41). This study was carried out within the PE1 - FAIR (Future Artificial Intelligence Research) and PE11 - MICS (Made in Italy - Circular and Sustainable) - European Union Next-Generation-EU (Piano Nazionale di Ripresa e Resilienza - PNRR). The work of Flavia Monti is supported by the MISE agreement on "Promozione del progetto della Scuola europea di industrial engineering and management e il sostegno di progetti innovativi di formazione in industrial engineering e management di impresa".

References

1. Amari, S.V., McLaughlin, L., Pham, H.: Cost-effective condition-based maintenance using Markov decision processes. In: RAMS, pp. 464–469. IEEE (2006)
2. Bicocchi, N., Cabri, G., Mandreoli, F., Mecella, M.: Dynamic digital factories for
   agile supply chains: an architectural approach. J. Ind. Inf. Integr. **15**, 111–121
   (2019)
3. Brafman, R.I., De Giacomo, G., Mecella, M., Sardina, S.: Service composition in
   stochastic settings. In: Esposito, F., Basili, R., Ferilli, S., Lisi, F. (eds.) AIxIA
   2017. ecture Notes in Computer Science, vol. 10640, pp. 159–171. Springer, Cham
   (2017). https://doi.org/10.1007/978-3-319-70169-1_12
4. Catarci, T., Firmani, D., Leotta, F., Mandreoli, F., Mecella, M., Sapio, F.: A
   conceptual architecture and model for smart manufacturing relying on service-
   based digital twins. In: IEEE ICWS, pp. 229–236 (2019)
5. Choo, B.Y., Adams, S.C., Weiss, B.A., Marvel, J.A., Beling, P.A.: Adaptive multi-
   scale prognostics and health management for smart manufacturing systems. Int.
   J. Prognostics Health Manage. **7** (2016)
6. De Giacomo, G., Favorito, M.: Compositional approach to translate LTLf/LDLf
   into deterministic finite automata. In: ICAPS, pp. 122–130. AAAI Press (2021)
7. De Giacomo, G., Favorito, M., Leotta, F., Mecella, M., Silo, L.: Digital twins
   composition in smart manufacturing via Markov decision processes. Comput. Ind.
   149, 103916 (2023)
8. De Giacomo, G., Vardi, M.Y.: Linear temporal logic and linear dynamic logic on
   finite traces. In: IJCAI, pp. 854–860. ACM (2013)
9. Dumas, M., et al.: AI-augmented business process management systems: a research
   manifesto. ACM Trans. Manage. Inf. Syst. **14**(1), 1–19 (2023)
10. Han, H., Trimi, S.: Towards a data science platform for improving SME collab-
    oration through Industry 4.0 technologies. Technol. Forecast. Soc. Change **174**,
    121242 (2022)
11. Hu, H., Jia, X., Liu, K., Sun, B.: Self-adaptive traffic control model with behavior
    trees and reinforcement learning for AGV in industry 4.0. IEEE Trans. Ind. Inf.
    17(12), 7968–7979 (2021)
12. Liu, Z., et al.: The architectural design and implementation of a digital platform
    for industry 4.0 SME collaboration. Comput. Ind. **138**, 103623 (2022)
13. Marrella, A., Mecella, M., Pernici, B., Plebani, P.: A design-time data-centric matu-
    rity model for assessing resilience in multi-party business processes. Inf. Syst. **86**,
    62–78 (2019)
14. Marrella, A., Mecella, M., Sardina, S.: SmartPM: an adaptive process management
    system through situation calculus, IndiGolog, and classical planning. In: KR (2014)
15. Pesic, M., Schonenberg, H., Van der Aalst, W.M.: Declare: Full support for loosely-
    structured processes. In: EDOC, pp. 287–287. IEEE (2007)
16. Popkova, E.G., Ragulina, Y.V., Bogoviz, A.V. (eds.): Industry 4.0: Industrial Rev-
    olution of the 21st Century. SSDC, vol. 169. Springer, Cham (2019). https://doi.
    org/10.1007/978-3-319-94310-7
17. Puterman, M.L.: Markov Decision Processes. Wiley, Hoboken (1994)
18. Rocchetta, R., Bellani, L., Compare, M., Zio, E., Patelli, E.: A reinforcement learn-
    ing framework for optimal operation and maintenance of power grids. Appl. Energy
    241, 291–301 (2019)
19. Sahal, R., Breslin, J.G., Ali, M.I.: Big data and stream processing platforms for
    Industry 4.0 requirements mapping for a predictive maintenance use case. J. Manuf.
    Syst. **54**, 138–151 (2020)

20. Terkaj, W., Tolio, T., Urgo, M.: A virtual factory approach for in situ simulation to support production and maintenance planning. CIRP Ann. **64**(1), 451–454 (2015)
21. Wally, B., et al.: Leveraging iterative plan refinement for reactive smart manufacturing systems. IEEE Trans. Autom. Sci. Eng. **18**, 230–243 (2020)
22. Wray, K.H., Zilberstein, S., Mouaddib, A.I.: Multi-objective MDPs with conditional lexicographic reward preferences. In: AAAI (2015)
23. Zahoransky, R.M., Brenig, C., Koslowski, T.: Towards a process-centered resilience framework. In: ARES, pp. 266–273. IEEE (2015)
24. Zahoransky, R.M., Koslowski, T., Accorsi, R.: Toward resilience assessment in business process architectures. In: Bondavalli, A., Ceccarelli, A., Ortmeier, F. (eds.) SAFECOMP 2014. LNCS, vol. 8696, pp. 360–370. Springer, Cham (2014). https://doi.org/10.1007/978-3-319-10557-4_39

Conceptual Formalization of Massive Storage for Advancing Decision-Making with Data Analytics

Vânia Sousa[1,2](✉) [iD], Daniela Barros[1,2] [iD], Pedro Guimarães[1,2] [iD],
Antonina Santos[3] [iD], and Maribel Yasmina Santos[2] [iD]

[1] Computer Graphics Centre, Campus de Azurém, 4800-058 Guimarães, Portugal
{daniela.barros,pedro.guimaraes}@ccg.pt
[2] ALGORITMI Research Centre, University of Minho, Campus de Azurém,
4800-058 Guimarães, Portugal
pg30061@alunos.uminho.pt, maribel@dsi.uminho.pt
[3] Sonae Arauco Deutschland GmbH, Maia, Portugal
antonina.santos@sonaearauco.com

Abstract. Data Lakes have been widely used to handle massive amounts of data arriving at high velocity and variety. However, if proper data management concerns are not addressed, this massive data storage can easily turn Data Lakes into Data Swamps. Furthermore, data must be associated with the data artefacts created to extract value from it, such as pipelines used to collect, treat, or process data and analytical artefacts such as analytical dashboards and machine learning models. This paper proposes a more comprehensive view of a Data Lake, in which all of these resources can be stored and managed. To that end, the conceptual meta-model incorporates a data catalog, data at various stages of maturity, pipelines, dashboards, and machine learning models. The proposed meta-model was instantiated in the ADM.IN (Advanced Decision Making in Productive Systems through Intelligent Networks) project, showing how vast amounts of data and their related artefacts can be managed to support decision-making processes with data analytics.

Keywords: Big Data Analytics · Data Lake · Productive Systems

1 Introduction

Big Data has received increasing attention over the years, and as a result, numerous techniques and tools for Big Data Analytics (BDA) have been developed. These techniques and tools are increasingly used to support decision-making because it is necessary to transform raw data into useful business information [8], and thus capitalize on the strategic potential of large amounts of data provided by organizations. To support data needs, a BDA system that integrates components for data collection, storage, processing, analysis, and distribution of valuable information to stakeholders is required [9]. Data Lakes are a type of storage component that can be used in BDA systems.

According to [10], *"a data lake is a scalable and analysis system for data of any type, retained in their native format and used mainly by data specialists for knowledge extraction"*. The authors also state that Data Lakes include a metadata catalog, data governance policies and tools, accessibility to various kinds of users, integration of any type of data, a logical and physical organization, and scalability in terms of storage and processing. There are numerous ways to organize a Data Lake and structure how data are stored and made available to users, each one with distinct advantages. However, without proper architecture and metadata management, a Data Lake can quickly become a Data Swamp, that is, an inoperable Data Lake [6,10]. There are two types of Data Lake architectures: data pond and zone architectures [2,10]. In data pond architectures, data are distributed across ponds, which may be viewed as a subset of the Data Lake containing data of a particular type and that are available only in one pond at any given point in time [2,10]. In zone architectures, data are categorized into zones based on how much processing they have gone through [2].

This paper proposes a more comprehensive view of a Data Lake in which all resources can be stored and managed in a zone architecture. To that end, a conceptual meta-model for the storage system is proposed, which includes storage areas concerned not only with data at various stages of maturity, but also with all of the resources needed to manage these data, such as pipelines, machine learning (ML) models, and dashboards. Furthermore, the Governance Area is taken into account for the efficient management of the storage system's available resources.

The remainder of this paper is organized as follows: Sect. 2 discusses previous research on the subject. The proposed conceptual Data Lake's architecture and meta-model are presented in Sect. 3. In Sect. 4, a demonstration case of the proposed architecture is shown. Section 5 summarizes the proposed work and outlines future research directions.

2   Related Work

Several approaches for structuring Data Lakes are described in the literature, mainly organized in ponds or in zones [2,10], as mentioned above. [5] presents a data pond architecture. The author suggests the existence of five distinct ponds: the Raw Data Pond, the Analog Data Pond, the Application Data Pond, the Textual Data Pond, and the Archival Data Pond. Raw data that are pre-processed can be used for further analyses. However, raw data are deleted once the pre-processed data are moved to another pond, which means that the detailed raw data are lost.

In the works of [3] and [11], the authors assume the existence of a Landing Zone/Transient Landing Zone in which raw data are accessible. The work of [7] only considers the existence of the Raw Zone, where raw data are stored. There are architectures, such as [4], that name the first zone as Raw/Landing and are quite similar to the design presented in [7]. When it comes to cleaning and storing the processed data, [4] considers the Gold/Production Zone and [7] the Process

Zone, while [3] considers the Harmonized Zone and [11] the Trusted Zone. [4] suggests the Dev/Work Zone, [7] suggests the Access Zone, and [3] suggests the Destilled Zone for keeping and making data available for analysis. On this point, [11] suggests the Refined Zone, where data access is restricted to certain users. [3] also proposes that data scientists have restricted access to the data within the Explorative Zone. This author also proposes the existence of a Delivery Zone that is similar to the Explorative Zone, but with additional access permissions. The main differences between the presented architectures are the presence of a Sensitive Zone in [4] and a Sandbox in [11] that provides a testing environment where data can be accessed without limitation. Although Data Lake governance is already an issue in [11], only [7] suggests the development of a Governance Zone used for data management, focusing mainly on ensuring security, quality, life cycle and access to data. Moreover, it is responsible for managing metadata.

There have already been concerns about metadata management, as it can reduce the risk of losing data control. [1] proposes MOSES, a framework for managing metadata in Big Data platforms, with a metadata repository as its primary component. Although the authors present a meta-model of MOSES and acknowledge that it is useful for tracking data, data-related resources like dashboards, ML models, and pipelines are not here considered.

Despite the relevance of these works in proposing ways to organize a Data Lake, these approaches do not address the storage of data and their related artefacts following the principles proposed in this paper, as described next.

3   Conceptual Data Lake's Architecture and Meta-Model

As shown in the previous section, there are several potential architectures for Data Lakes, but none of them addresses the several components proposed here, with concerns with data and the related data artefacts. This is a key issue in data engineering, as an adequate architecture is mandatory to prevent Data Lakes from becoming Data Swamps [6]. Since several data providers and consumers can access a Data Lake, rather than just data engineers, it is crucial that these architectures are organized in an appropriate and intuitive manner, and are easily accessible, so that data providers and consumers, regardless of their technical expertise, can understand where the resources are stored and why. The proposal here presented considers three storage zones for data at different maturity stages along with their related artefacts, Bronze Zone, Silver Zone and Gold Zone, and one additional zone for governance, Platinum Zone. A general architecture is depicted in Fig. 1, as a possible instantiation of the meta-model proposed afterwards, highlighting the four storage zones and their components. This instance is presented first to provide a general overview of the proposal.

In the Bronze Zone, data are available in their source formats and usually with a high level of detail. Pipelines for collecting and storing these data are also here available. The underlying principle is to maintain data as close as possible to their related data artefacts. In the Silver Zone, data was already processed, filtered, aggregated, and tested to fulfil the specified quality criteria. Besides the pipelines developed to perform such data operations, this zone also stores any malformed data found in the preparation process. This is important to identify the main data problems and devise strategies for improving data quality.

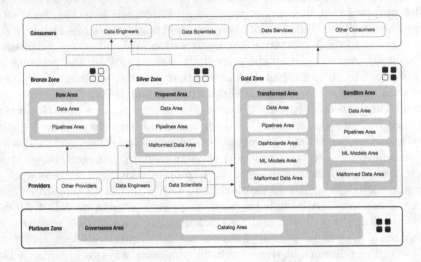

Fig. 1. Possible Data Lake Architecture.

As can be seen in Fig. 1, malformed data can be identified at different phases of the data life cycle, reason why the proposed architecture foresees different storage areas for them in case they are needed. In the Gold Zone, data already transformed and ready to be used in data analytics tasks or by ML techniques are available. Besides the pipelines and any identified malformed data, the Transformed Area includes the storage of the dashboards developed for analytics, as well as any identified ML models. To allow data scientists to perform exploratory data analytics, the SandBox Area can be used for training ML algorithms. The Platinum Zone ensures that both data and data artefacts are catalogued, secure, private, accessible, and usable. Different data providers may interact with the Data Lake's zones, making available data and related resources. The same happens with data consumers, depending on the data consumer type. As previously stated, this architecture represents a possible instantiation of the meta-model proposed in this work to organize massive data storage and related resources. Data and their various stages of maturity are central to this meta-model. The maturity stages can be classified into types, for instance low, medium, and high. Different pipelines may be developed to address the evolution of data along these different maturity stages. Figure 2 depicts this component of the meta-model and the relationships between Data and Pipelines.

Addressing the Data Lake as a whole (Fig. 3), it includes several Storage Areas, in which all the resources may be organized by Domains. These can group data sets and their related data artefacts by business processes, application domains, or any other approach that fits the Data Lake purpose. Several data providers and consumers (Data Provider/Consumer) can feed the storage system or use its available resources. Besides the pipelines to handle data, several Dashboards or ML Models can make available analytical artefacts that are relevant for decision support. All these resources have the associated Metadata that are integrated into the Governance Catalog.

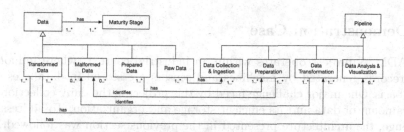

Fig. 2. Conceptualization of Data and Pipelines.

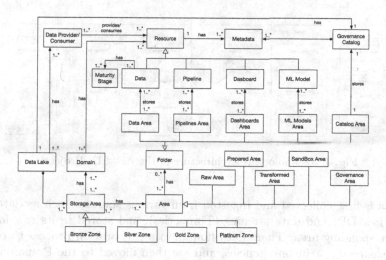

Fig. 3. Meta-model for the Data Lake Storage System.

As previously mentioned, the Storage Areas can be specialized into four different zones. The Governance Area associated with the Platinum Zone stores the catalog used to manage all the available resources. The Raw Area included in the Bronze Zone has the data and corresponding resources, such as pipelines. The Prepared Area included in the Silver Zone stores the prepared data, pipelines and, for instance, any identified malformed data. The Transformed Area included in the Gold Zone stores data and all their related artefacts - pipelines, dashboards and ML models - besides any identified malformed data if this is relevant at this stage of the data life cycle. This zone also includes the SandBox Area for exploratory data analysis with ML, storing the data, ML models, and any identified malformed data (if needed). The instantiation of this meta-model into a folder structure for the Data Lake makes it feasible to know where a resource is available. This ensures that the Data Lake remains organized over time, preventing it from becoming a Data Swamp.

4   Demonstration Case

The ADM.IN project operates within an industrial context, where millions of data records generated by machines and sensors are stored in databases on a daily basis. One major challenge faced by this project is the daily collection of a large amount of data and its efficient storage and organization. To address this challenge, the architecture presented in the previous section was followed. The Data Lake not only stores data coming from the factory, but also pipeline scripts, ML models, and dashboards. These resources are stored in different maturity zones based on their level of processing and transformation. The technological architecture implemented in the ADM.IN project is depicted in Fig. 4.

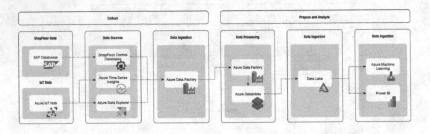

Fig. 4. Technological Architecture of the ADM.IN Project.

Data is first collected and ingested from various sources, such as databases (ShopFloor DB) and data streams (Timeseries), and stored in its raw form in the corresponding area. Then, data flows into a preparation process to remove any inaccuracies or inconsistencies, and are then moved to the Prepared Data Area. In this area, data are transformed and optimized for specific use cases, such as implementing analytical dashboards or training ML models. The transformed data are then stored in the Transformed Data Area, while the analytical dashboards and ML models are stored, respectively, in Dashboards Area and ML Models Area (Fig. 5). With the adoption of this approach, the Data Lake is enhanced, leading to increased efficiency and support for effective data management. The comprehensive understanding of the data location minimizes the possibility of errors and reduces the time required for data engineers and scientists to locate the necessary data to develop artefacts.

For instance, dedicating a specific storage location for a dashboard's data enhances the development process, as all the required data are located within a

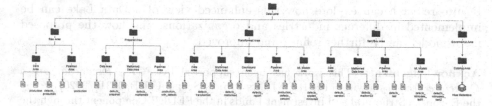

Fig. 5. Data Lake Architecture Implemented in the ADM.IN Project.

single and easily identifiable area. The dashboard depicted in Fig. 6 integrates several graphs from different tables, all of them stored in the Dashboards Area. This principle enables simplified management of the dashboard, as each table handles a specific indicator, such as the most frequently detected product defects in the production process.

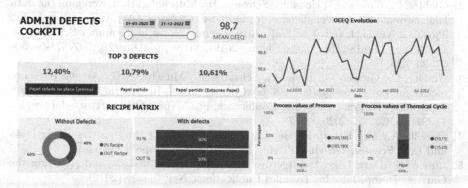

Fig. 6. Defects Dashboard of the ADM.IN Project.

5 Conclusions

This paper has discussed the potential of Data Lakes as a storage component in BDA systems, as well as the challenges associated with managing large amounts of data without a proper architecture and metadata management. The proposed meta-model for a Data Lake enhances its capabilities by integrating storage areas for data at different maturity stages, as well as artefacts such as pipelines, ML models, and dashboards, all of which can be managed through a governance area for efficient resource management. By adopting this enhanced view of a Data Lake, organizations can better manage their data resources and extract more value from their data, supporting decision-making processes with data analytics. The ADM.IN project is an example of how this meta-model can be effectively instantiated to manage large amounts of data and related artefacts.

Future research can explore how this enhanced view of a Data Lake can be implemented in different industries and organizations, and how the proposed meta-model can be further refined and improved.

Acknowledgements. This work has been supported by *FCT - Fundação para a Ciência e Tecnologia* within the R&D Units Project Scope: UIDB/00319/2020, and by the European Structural and Investment Funds in the FEDER Component through the Operational Competitiveness and Internationalization Programme (COMPETE 2020) under Advanced Decision Making in productive systems through Intelligent Networks (ADM.IN) Project 055087 (POCI-01-0247-FEDER-055087).

References

1. Francia, M., Gallinucci, E., Golfarelli, M., Giulia, A., Rizzi, S., Santolini, N.: Making data platforms smarter with MOSES. Future Gener. Comput. Syst. **125**, 299–313 (2021). https://doi.org/10.1016/j.future.2021.06.031
2. Giebler, C., Gröger, C., Hoos, E., Schwarz, H., Mitschang, B.: Leveraging the data lake: current state and challenges. In: Ordonez, C., Song, I.Y., Anderst-Kotsis, G., Tjoa, A., Khalil, I. (eds.) DaWaK 2019. Lecture Notes in Computer Science, vol. 11708, pp. 179–188. Springer, Cham (2019). https://doi.org/10.1007/978-3-030-27520-4_13
3. Giebler, C., Groger, C., Hoos, E., Schwarz, H., Mitschang, B.: A zone reference model for enterprise-grade data lake management. In: International Enterprise Distributed Object Computing Conference, pp. 57–66 (2020). https://doi.org/10.1109/EDOC49727.2020.00017
4. Gorelik, A.: The Enterprise Big Data Lake: Delivering the Promise of Big Data and Data Science, 1st edn. O'Reilly Media Inc, Sebastopol (2019)
5. Inmon, B.: Data Lake Architecture: Designing the Data Lake and Avoiding the Garbage Dump, 1st edn. Technics Publications, New Jersey (2016)
6. Nargesian, F., Zhu, E., Miller, R.J., Pu, K.Q., Arocena, P.C.: Data lake management: Challenges and opportunities. Proc. VLDB Endowment **12**(12), 1986–1989 (2018). https://doi.org/10.14778/3352063.3352116
7. Ravat, F., Zhao, Y.: Data lakes: trends and perspectives. In: Hartmann, S., Küng, J., Chakravarthy, S., Anderst-Kotsis, G., Tjoa, A.M., Khalil, I. (eds.) DEXA 2019. LNCS, vol. 11706, pp. 304–313. Springer, Cham (2019). https://doi.org/10.1007/978-3-030-27615-7_23
8. Sabharwal, R., Miah, S.J.: A new theoretical understanding of big data analytics capabilities in organizations: a thematic analysis. J. Big Data **8**(1), 1–17 (2021). https://doi.org/10.1186/s40537-021-00543-6
9. Santos, M.Y., et al.: A big data system supporting Bosch Braga industry 4.0 strategy. Int. J. Inf. Manage. **37**(6), 750–760 (2017). https://doi.org/10.1016/j.ijinfomgt.2017.07.012
10. Sawadogo, P., Darmont, J.: On data lake architectures and metadata management. J. Intell. Inf. Syst. **56**(1), 97–120 (2020). https://doi.org/10.1007/s10844-020-00608-7
11. Sharma, B.: Architecting Data Lakes - Data Management Architectures for Advanced Business Use Cases, 2nd edn. O'Reilly Media Inc, Sebastopol (2018)

Towards Leveraging Tests to Identify Impacts of Metamodel and Code Co-evolution

Zohra Kaouter Kebaili[1]([✉]), Djamel Eddine Khelladi[1], Mathieu Acher[2], and Olivier Barais[3]

[1] CNRS, Univ. Rennes 1, IRISA, INRIA, Rennes, France
{zohra-kaouter.kebaili,djamel-eddine.khelladi}@irisa.fr
[2] INSA, IUF, IRISA, Inria, Rennes, France
mathieu.acher@irisa.fr
[3] Univ. Rennes 1, IRISA, INRIA, Rennes, France
olivier.barais@irisa.fr

Abstract. Models play a significant role in Model-Driven Engineering (MDE) and metamodels are commonly transformed into code. Developers intensively rely on the generated code to build language services and tooling, such as editors and views which are also tested to ensure their behavior. The metamodel evolution between releases updates the generated code, and this may impact the developers' additional, client code. Accordingly, the impacted code must be co-evolved too, but there is no guarantee of preserving its behavior correctness. This paper envisions an automatic approach for ensuring code co-evolution correctness. It first aims to trace the tests impacted by the metamodel evolution before and after the code co-evolution, and then compares them to analyze the behavior of the code. Preliminary evaluation on two implementations of OCL and Modisco Eclipse projects. Showed that we can successfully traced the impacted tests automatically by selecting 738 and 412 tests, before and after co-evolution respectively, based on 303 metamodel changes. By running these impacted tests, we observed both behaviorally correct and incorrect code co-evolution.

Keywords: Model evolution · Code co-evolution · Unit tests · Testing co-evolution

1 Introduction

Model-driven engineering (MDE) is a software engineering approach to help and support the construction and maintenance of large-scale systems [8,9,13]. MDE promotes the use of models as first-class entities during the development lifecycle of a system. Models that conform to *metamodels* are used as inputs of code generators that leverage the abstract, domain-specific concepts. For example, the JHipster project is adopted in 344 companies[1] and proposes to generate, from

---

[1] https://www.jhipster.tech/companies-using-jhipster/.

C. Cabanillas and F. Perez (Eds.): CAiSE 2023, LNBIP 477, pp. 129–137, 2023.
https://doi.org/10.1007/978-3-031-34674-3_16

entity models, the different stacks of modern web applications for both client- and server-side code. Another popular example is OpenAPI[2], where many artifacts are generated from an API specification. Some low-code development platforms rely on some of the MDE principles [4], with data models and generators to raise abstraction and hide implementation-level details. *Eclipse Modeling Framework (EMF)* [27] is another prominent example. Based on a *metamodel*, EMF generates Java code API, adapters, and an editor. This generated code is further enriched by developers to offer additional functionalities and tooling, such as validation, simulation, or debugging.

One of the problems developers face in *MDE* – and in the different technologies previously mentioned – is the impact of the evolution of metamodels on its dependent artifacts. in this paper we focus on the impact on code. Indeed, when a metamodel evolves between two releases, and as the core API is re-generated again, the additional code can be impacted. As a consequence, it must be co-evolved by the developers in the next release. However, developers should spend significant effort to ensure that the code co-evolution is behaviorally correct, i.e., without altering the behavior of their impacted code. Whereas several existing approaches automate metamodels and code co-evolution [11,12,17,25,26,30,31], to the best of our knowledge, they do not focus on checking the behavioral correctness of the co-evolved code.

This paper envisions a new fully automatic approach to check the behavioral correctness of the metamodel and code co-evolution between different releases of a language, i.e., when the metamodel evolves. Our key idea is to leverage the test suites of the original and evolved versions of the metamodel. Specifically, the approach first takes as input the metamodel changes and then locates all usages of the metamodel change elements in the generated code. After that, we recursively trace the code usages until we reach the test methods. Thus, we end up matching the metamodel changes with impacted code methods and their corresponding tests. We perform this step on both original and evolved releases to check the behavioral correctness of the code before and after co-evolution.

We ran a preliminary evaluated with a prototype implementation on 2 Eclipse projects from the implementations of OCL and Modisco over several evolved versions of metamodels. As we did not find manually written tests in those projects, we generate a test suite for each release with the best available state-of-the-art tool EvoSuite [5]. Preliminary results show that we can automatically select respectively in the original and evolved releases 738 and 412 tests based on 303 metamodel changes. When running the traced tests before and after co-evolution, we could observe two cases indicating possibly both behaviorally incorrect and correct code co-evolution. Thus, helping the developer to locate the co-evolved code that must be investigated in more detail. The rest of the paper is structured as follows. Section 2 presents our envisioned approach for test tracing, while Sect. 3 describes the preliminary evaluation. Section 4 discusses the related work. Finally, Sect. 5 concludes the paper and discusses future work.

---

[2] https://oai.github.io/Documentation/.

2   Envisioned Approach

This section presents our proposed envisioned generic approach for tracing model evolution to tests. First, it provides an overview. Then, it describes how to handle the model changes and how to trace their impacts until the tests.

2.1   Overview

Figure 1 represents the overall approach workflow. First, we compute the difference between the two model versions (step $\boxed{1}$). In the original version, the additional code is the impacted one, and in the evolved version, the additional code is the co-evolved one. After that, we run the impact and the test tracing analysis (step $\boxed{2}$). Therefore, the developer can run the tests before and after the code co-evolution to check the behavioral correctness of the co-evolved code.

2.2   Detection of Model Changes

Several existing approaches allow to detect model changes between two versions, such as [3,18,19,22,28,29]. In Fig. 1, step $\boxed{1}$, we use a change interface as input to our test tracing approach. The change interface is a specification layer for the detected changes between two versions. Therefore, any detection approach [3,15, 19,22,28,29] can be integrated by bridging its changes to our change interface and the rest of our approach can be performed independently.

Taking into account both *atomic* (e.g., adds, deletes) and *complex* (e.g., move, split) changes [7], the list of impacting model changes [3,10] we consider to trace the tests is as follows: *1)* Delete property p in a class C. *2)* Delete class C. *3)* Rename element e in a class C. *4)* Generalize property p multiplicity from a single value to multiple values in a class C. *5)* Move property p from class S to T through a reference *ref.* *6)* Extract class of properties $p_1, ..., p_n$ from S to T through a reference *ref.* *7)* Push property p from super class Sup to sub classes $Sub_1,...,Sub_n$. *8)* Inline class S to T with properties $p_1, ..., p_n$. *9)* Change property p type from S to T in a class C. These changes were selected after observing many versions of evolving of various types of models [20,21].

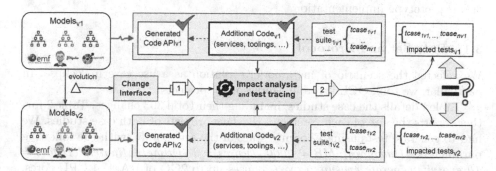

Fig. 1. Overall envisioned approach.

2.3   Tracing the Impacted Tests

Algorithm 1 describes how to check the behavioral correctness of the code co-evolution, by tracing the impact of model changes up to the test. To do that, we structure the code source to better navigate in it. Before starting Algorithm 1, we must parse the code source including tests and build the code Methods Call Graph (MCG), to retrieve the calling methods of the method invocations. Hence, trace the methods' calls recursively up to the tests. First, for each model change, we identify the list of code usages of the evolved model element. (Line 1). For example, when renaming a property called *name*, the algorithm will first find its usages, such as *getName()* or *setName()*. Then, in Line 5 we filter these impacted code usages by keeping only the ones found inside a Method Declaration, we will call this impacted method declaration *IMD*.s or if it is already treated. Therefore, after browsing all the impacted code usages, Algorithm 1 traces the list of all impacted tests, if any. For example, Listing 1.1 presents an impacted test due to a property type changing. After detecting that the type of the attribute *stereotype* is set from *Type* to *Stereotype* in the class *ElementExtension*, Algorithm 1 detects the code usage *stereotype0*. After that, it traces it to the method *test003*. As it has the *@Test* annotation, we conclude that *test003* is an impacted test due to the detected set property type. After isolating the impacted tests before and after the co-evolution, the developer can run them to investigate their results (see Sect. 3.2).

Listing 1.1. Excerpt of an impacted test in pivot project.

```
1    @Test(timeout = 4000)
2    public void test003()   throws Throwable  {
3        ...
4      Stereotype stereotype0)= elementExtensionImpl0.basicGetStereotype();
5      assertNull(stereotype0.getName());
6    }
```

3   Preliminary Evaluation

This section presents the protocol and the results of our preliminary evaluation of our prototype implementation.

3.1   Data Set and Protocol

We selected the scenario of metamodel evolution as a use case in Eclipse. In particular, we took OCL [24] and Modisco [23] projects.

Table 1 details the case studies, including their total 303 changes. Table 2 further reports the size of each version of the Java projects of both case studies. We had to generate tests using EvoSuite state-of-the-art tool [5], with the following parameters: *-DmemoryInMB = 2000 -Dcores = 4 -DtimeInMinutesPerClass = 10 evosuite:generate evosuite:export*. It uses up to 2GO of RAM, 4 CPU cores, and 10 min per test class.

Algorithm 1: Impacted tests detection

Data: methodsCallGraph, change
1 impactedUsages ← match(AST, change)
2 impactedTests ← φ
3 **for** *(impactedUsage ∈ impactedUsages)* **do**
4 | /* Find the method declaration using impactedUsage*/
5 | IMD ← getIMD(impactedUsage, methodsCallGraph)
6 | **if** *(isTest(IMD))* **then**
7 | | impactedTests.add(IMD) /*If not already added*/
8 | **else**
9 | | parentsOfIMD ← getParents(IMD, methodsCallGraph)
10 | | nextRound.add(parentsOfIMD)
11 | | **while** *(nextRound.hasNewIMDs())* **do**
12 | | | IM ← nextRound.get()
13 | | | **if** *(isTest(IMD))* **then**
14 | | | | impactedTests.add(IMD)/*If not already added*/
15 | | | **else**
16 | | | | parentsOfIMD ← getParents(IMD, methodsCallGraph)
17 | | | | nextRound.add(parentsOfIMD)
18 | | **end**
19 **end**
20 **return** impactedTests

Table 1. Details of the metamodels and their evolutions.

Evolved metamodels	Versions	Atomic changes in the metamodel	Complex changes in the metamodel
Pivot.ecore in project *ocl.examples.pivot*	3.2.2 to 3.4.4	*Deletes:* 2 classes, 16 properties, 6 super types *Renames:* 1 class, 5 properties *Property changes:* 4 types; 2 multiplicities *Adds:* 25 classes, 121 properties, 36 super types	1 pull property 2 push properties
Benchmark.ecore in project *modisco.infra.discovery.benchmark*	0.9.0 to 0.13.0	*Deletes:* 6 classes, 19 properties, 5 super types *Renames:* 5 properties *Adds:* 7 classes, 24 properties, 4 super types	4 moves property 6 pull property 1 extract class 1 extract super class

3.2   Preliminary Results

With our prototype implementation, we could trace tests successfully with a total of 738 (9.4%) and 412 (7.3%) tests in the original and evolved versions, respectively, due to 303 metamodel changes. Thus, we can isolate for the developers the tests that must be executed and looked at to check the behavioral correctness of the co-evolution. Naturally, when the number of evolution changes increases, the number of tests we trace increases as well. Moreover, as several delete classes and properties occurred in the evolution changes, several tests are not generated in the evolved version, which explains why we trace more tests in the original version than in the evolved version. After tracing the tests, we could execute them to observe their effect before and after co-evolution of the

Table 2. Details of the projects and their tests.

Projects to co-evolve in response to the evolved metamodels	N^{o} of packages	N^{o} of classes	N^{o} of test packages	N^{o} of test classes	N^{o} of LOC	N^{o} of tests
$[P1_{V1}]$ ocl.examples.pivot	22	439	22	290	74002	7322
$[P1_{V2}]$ ocl.examples.pivot	22	480	22	220	89449	4990
$[P2_{V1}]$ org.eclipse.modisco. infra.discovery.benchmark	3	28	3	15	2333	524
$[P2_{V2}]$ org.eclipse.modisco. infra.discovery.benchmark	3	30	3	15	2588	619

Table 3. Selected tests before and after code co-evolution.

Projects	N^{o} pass	N^{o} fail	N^{o} error	Total
$[P1_{V1}]$ to $[P1_{V2}]$	106–97	2–5	347–192	455–294
$[P2_{V1}]$ to $[P2_{V2}]$	206–68	1–0	76–50	283–118

code, as shown in Table 3. In $[P1]$, even though the number of impacted tests decreased by 161, the number of passing tests decreased only by 9. Whereas the error tests decreased by 155, but, the failing tests increased by 3 from 2 to 5. This could indicate a behaviorally incorrect co-evolution. Moreover, in the other project $[P2]$, many tests that existed in the original version were not in the evolved version due to the delete changes of the metamodels, which is a sign of behavioral correct co-evolution, as the tests should be removed following the removal of the metamodel elements. These results aims to help developers to further check the code co-evolution rather than simply accepting them.

4   Related Work

This section discusses the main related work w.r.t. testing the (meta)model and the code co-evolution. Several approaches propose to automate metamodel co-evolution. Riedl et al. [26] propose an approach to detect inconsistencies between UML models and code. Pham et al. [25] propose an approach to synchronize architectural models and code with bidirectional mappings. Jongeling et al. [11, 12] propose an approach for the consistency checking between system models and their implementations by focusing on recovering the traceability links between the models and the code. Zaheri et al. [31] also propose to support the checking of the consistency-breaking updates between models and generated artifacts, including the code. Khelladi et al. [16,17] propose an approach that propagates the metamodel changes to the code as a co-evolution mechanism. However, all these approaches focus on co-evolving the code without checking the behavioral correctness of the co-evolved code. Ge et al. [6] propose to verify the correctness of refactoring with a set of condition checkers that are executed only after the refactoring application. However, our work is the first attempt that relies on a testing technique to check the behavioral correctness of the code co-evolution with the metamodel evolution.

5 Conclusion

This paper envisions an automated tracing of the impacted tests due to model evolution. By tracing the tests before and after code co-evolution, we must be able to check its behavioral correctness. We ran a preliminary evaluation on two implementations of OCL and Modisco metamodels containing generated tests with EvoSuite. Preliminary results show that we could traced 738 and 412 impacted tests based on the 303 metamodel changes. When running the traced tests before and after co-evolution, we could observe possibly both behaviorally incorrect and correct code co-evolution. This can help the developers to locate the suspicious co-evolved code. As future work, we plan to evaluate our approach on more Eclipse projects and on other case studies, such as to JHipster and OpenAPI which both generate code from a model specification similar to a metamodel. In future, we could also complement tests with formal verification, such as in [2,14] and build analyzing the build results or failures [1] before and after co-evolution.

Acknowledgement. The research leading to these results has received funding from the *ANR* agency under grant *ANR JCJC MC-EVO² 204687*.

References

1. Acher, M., Martin, H., Pereira, J.A., Blouin, A., Khelladi, D.E., Jézéquel, J.M.: Learning from thousands of build failures of Linux kernel configurations. Technical report (2019)
2. Chong, N., et al.: Code-level model checking in the software development workflow. In: The 42nd ICSE: SEIP, pp. 11–20 (2020)
3. Cicchetti, A., Di Ruscio, D., Pierantonio, A.: Managing dependent changes in coupled evolution. In: Paige, R.F. (ed.) ICMT 2009. LNCS, vol. 5563, pp. 35–51. Springer, Heidelberg (2009). https://doi.org/10.1007/978-3-642-02408-5_4
4. Di Ruscio, D., Kolovos, D., de Lara, J., Pierantonio, A., Tisi, M., Wimmer, M.: Low-code development and model-driven engineering: two sides of the same coin? Softw. Syst. Model. **21**(2), 437–446 (2022). https://doi.org/10.1007/s10270-021-00970-2
5. Fraser, G., Arcuri, A.: EvoSuite: automatic test suite generation for object-oriented software. In: Proceedings of the 19th ACM SIGSOFT Symposium and the 13th European Conference on Foundations of Software Engineering, pp. 416–419 (2011)
6. Ge, X., Murphy-Hill, E.: Manual refactoring changes with automated refactoring validation. In: Proceedings of the 36th International Conference on Software Engineering, pp. 1095–1105 (2014)
7. Herrmannsdoerfer, M., Vermolen, S.D., Wachsmuth, G.: An extensive catalog of operators for the coupled evolution of metamodels and models. In: Malloy, B., Staab, S., van den Brand, M. (eds.) SLE 2010. LNCS, vol. 6563, pp. 163–182. Springer, Heidelberg (2011). https://doi.org/10.1007/978-3-642-19440-5_10
8. Hutchinson, J., Rouncefield, M., Whittle, J.: Model-driven engineering practices in industry. In: Proceedings of the 33rd International Conference on Software Engineering, pp. 633–642. ACM (2011)

9. Hutchinson, J., Whittle, J., Rouncefield, M., Kristoffersen, S.: Empirical assessment of MDE in industry. In: Proceedings of the 33rd International Conference on Software Engineering, pp. 471–480. ACM (2011)

10. Iovino, L., Pierantonio, A., Malavolta, I.: On the impact significance of metamodel evolution in MDE. J. Object Technol. **11**(3), 3:1–3:33 (2012)

11. Jongeling, R., Fredriksson, J., Ciccozzi, F., Carlson, J., Cicchetti, A.: Structural consistency between a system model and its implementation: a design science study in industry. In: ECMFA (2022)

12. Jongeling, R., Fredriksson, J., Ciccozzi, F., Cicchetti, A., Carlson, J.: Towards consistency checking between a system model and its implementation. In: Babur, Ö., Denil, J., Vogel-Heuser, B. (eds.) ICSMM 2020. CCIS, vol. 1262, pp. 30–39. Springer, Cham (2020). https://doi.org/10.1007/978-3-030-58167-1_3

13. Kent, S.: Model driven engineering. In: Butler, M., Petre, L., Sere, K. (eds.) IFM 2002. LNCS, vol. 2335, pp. 286–298. Springer, Heidelberg (2002). https://doi.org/10.1007/3-540-47884-1_16

14. Khelladi, D.E., Bendraou, R., Baarir, S., Laurent, Y., Gervais, M.P.: A framework to formally verify conformance of a software process to a software method. In: The 30th Symposium on Applied Computing, pp. 1518–1525. ACM (2015)

15. Khelladi, D.E., Bendraou, R., Gervais, M.P.: AD-ROOM: a tool for automatic detection of refactorings in object-oriented models. In: ICSE Companion, pp. 617–620. ACM (2016)

16. Khelladi, D.E., Combemale, B., Acher, M., Barais, O.: On the power of abstraction: a model-driven co-evolution approach of software code. In: 42nd International Conference on Software Engineering: New Ideas and Emerging Results (ICSE-NIER) (2020)

17. Khelladi, D.E., Combemale, B., Acher, M., Barais, O., Jézéquel, J.M.: Co-evolving code with evolving metamodels. In: Proceedings of the ACM/IEEE 42nd International Conference on Software Engineering, ICSE 2020, pp. 1496–1508 (2020)

18. Khelladi, D.E., Hebig, R., Bendraou, R., Robin, J., Gervais, M.-P.: Detecting complex changes during metamodel evolution. In: Zdravkovic, J., Kirikova, M., Johannesson, P. (eds.) CAiSE 2015. LNCS, vol. 9097, pp. 263–278. Springer, Cham (2015). https://doi.org/10.1007/978-3-319-19069-3_17

19. Khelladi, D.E., Hebig, R., Bendraou, R., Robin, J., Gervais, M.P.: Detecting complex changes and refactorings during (meta) model evolution. Inf. Syst. **62**, 220–241 (2016). https://doi.org/10.1016/j.is.2016.05.002

20. Khelladi, D.E., Kretschmer, R., Egyed, A.: Change propagation-based and composition-based co-evolution of transformations with evolving metamodels. In: Model Driven Engineering Languages and Systems, pp. 404–414. ACM (2018)

21. Kretschmer, R., Khelladi, D.E., Lopez-Herrejon, R.E., Egyed, A.: Consistent change propagation within models. Softw. Syst. Model. **20**, 539–555 (2021). https://doi.org/10.1007/s10270-020-00823-4

22. Langer, P., et al.: A posteriori operation detection in evolving software models. J. Syst. Softw. **86**(2), 551–566 (2013)

23. MDT: Model development tools. MoDisco (2015). http://www.eclipse.org/modeling/mdt/?project=modisco

24. MDT: Model development tools. object constraints language (OCL) (2015). http://www.eclipse.org/modeling/mdt/?project=ocl

25. Pham, V.C., Radermacher, A., Gerard, S., Li, S.: Bidirectional mapping between architecture model and code for synchronization. In: International Conference on Software Architecture (ICSA), pp. 239–242. IEEE (2017)

26. Riedl-Ehrenleitner, M., Demuth, A., Egyed, A.: Towards model-and-code consistency checking. In: COMPSAC, pp. 85–90. IEEE (2014)
27. Steinberg, D., Budinsky, F., Merks, E., Paternostro, M.: EMF: Eclipse Modeling Framework. Pearson Education (2008)
28. Vermolen, S.D., Wachsmuth, G., Visser, E.: Reconstructing complex metamodel evolution. In: Sloane, A., Aßmann, U. (eds.) SLE 2011. LNCS, vol. 6940, pp. 201–221. Springer, Heidelberg (2012). https://doi.org/10.1007/978-3-642-28830-2_11
29. Williams, J.R., Paige, R.F., Polack, F.A.: Searching for model migration strategies. In: Workshop on Models and Evolution, at MODELS, pp. 39–44. ACM (2012)
30. Yu, Y., Lin, Y., Hu, Z., Hidaka, S., Kato, H., Montrieux, L.: Maintaining invariant traceability through bidirectional transformations. In: 2012 34th International Conference on Software Engineering (ICSE), pp. 540–550. IEEE (2012)
31. Zaheri, M., Famelis, M., Syriani, E.: Towards checking consistency-breaking updates between models and generated artifacts. In: Model Driven Engineering Languages and Systems - Companion (MODELS-C), pp. 400–409. IEEE (2021)

Advancing IS Strategy for Natural History Museums with Method Engineering in the Digital Age

Cristabel Evelia Alvarado Pérez[1,2]([✉]) [iD], Eulàlia Garcia Franquesa[2] [iD], and Joan Antoni Pastor Collado[1] [iD]

[1] Universitat Politècnica de Catalunya, 08034 Barcelona, BA, Spain
`cristabel.alvarado@upc.edu, pastor@essi.upc.edu`
[2] Museu de Ciències Naturals de Barcelona, 08019 Barcelona, BA, Spain
`{calvarado,egarciafr}@bcn.cat`

Abstract. The evolution of information systems and technologies (IS/IT) has driven a fundamental transformation of services and processes within various types of organizations. Specifically, technologies such as AI, virtual reality, augmented reality, big data, drones, cloud, 3D printers and IoT have originated the phenomenon in literature known as digital transformation. Digital transformation (DT) is a strategic, organization-wide approach that brings together process, technology and people. It is not just a matter of technological investment, but of considering improved ways of implementing the organisation's mission, rethinking its core functions to benefit from digital. Over the last decades, museums have also been committed to digital innovation, although at a slower pace than other sectors, so that today many museums are still far from reaching a high level of digital maturity. In such circumstances, the strategic planning of DT and the right leadership for deploying digital projects, are crucial to establish guidelines, objectives and strategic projects that support the achievement of museum's mission and enhance their relevance in today's society. In order to explore such a strategic approach, the Museu de Ciències Naturals de Barcelona (MCNB) and the Universitat Politècnica de Catalunya (UPC) are cooperating in an applied research project, approved and funded by the Industrial Doctorate Programme of the Generalitat de Catalunya, resulting in a method for the strategic planning of DT initiatives in Natural History Museums, as well as the first DT plan for the collections area of the MCNB.

Keywords: IS/IT Strategic Planning · Digital Transformation · Method Design · Digital Museum · Natural History Museums · Cyber Human Systems

1 Introduction

Information systems and technology (IS/IT) strategy is of paramount importance and has been studied by numerous well-developed lines of research that have contributed to our understanding of IS/IT strategy. In recent decades, however, digitisation has fundamentally changed organisations and challenged traditional strategic wisdom. As a result, an evolutionary shift in IS/IT strategy thinking has also given rise to new terms such as digital transformation [1].

Digital transformation (DT) can be defined as an evolutionary process that leverages digital capabilities and technologies to enable business models, operational processes, and customer experiences to create value [2]. Therefore, DT is often a complicated process that involves not only the incorporation of digital technologies (AI, virtual reality, augmented reality, big data, drones, cloud, 3D printers and IoT) but also an eventual rethinking of processes, legacy systems and even organisational culture [3–5]. Consequently, DT is a major challenge for organisations today [6].

Heritage institutions face even more obstacles in their DT process. As defined by the International Council of Museums (ICOM), museums are non-profit organizations that serve society by collecting, researching, conserving, exhibiting and interpreting tangible and intangible heritage. A museum must be open to the public, accessible, inclusive, and provide diverse experiences for education, enjoyment, reflection and knowledge sharing [7]. It is therefore imperative that museums, as largely public institutions, maintain the link between themselves and their publics/audiences. On the one hand, this is an implicit part of their nature, core activities and mission; on the other hand, they need to remain relevant to 21st society in order to justify their existence and receive the necessary funding from the public authorities that govern them.

Paradoxically, the adoption of digital technology and the internet in the heritage sector has not been sudden, but has been a long and gradual process, spanning more than half a century [8]. In the early 1960s, the Smithsonian National Museum of Natural History began to explore the potential of collections management using computerised systems [8, 9]. Other museums also tried to do this at that time. By the 1980s, new technologies had been developed to support digital imaging, and museums began to build digital image databases. With the advent of the Internet, museum professionals found more ways to share data about their collections [9].

However, the process of digitisation in the museum sector has not always been supported and encouraged by staff due to undesirable outcomes such as loss of information in the migration of data from manual to automated systems. As a result, the heritage sector had to start from scratch, which further slowed the transition to digitisation. Furthermore, the high cost of using computers in relation to the modest resources typically available to museologists, together with resistance to the intrusion of IS/IT into their traditional roles, meant that museums were slow to realise the potential of technology as a research/education/communication tool. Today, the process of digitisation is considered a mandatory activity for cultural organisations [8].

DT has reshaped the entire museum experience and operation, providing a variety of ways to deliver information and share knowledge with the public. This alliance between IS/IT and cultural organisations has given rise to the term "digital museum", which refers to a museum that fully integrates digital tools into its working methods to enhance its core functions: collecting, conserving, researching, exhibiting and communicating [8, 10]. Although museums continue to embrace digital innovation, they are doing it more slowly than other sectors of society [11, 12]. As a consequence, many museums are still far from achieving a high level of digital maturity [12, 13].

While the relative scarcity of resources and staff availability in the cultural heritage sector may hinder DT in museums, such limitations can be better addressed with the right institutional leadership and the use of guidelines and methodologies specifically designed for the museum reality, allowing DT to be planned and addressed with a strategic, methodical, systematic and cross-cutting approach that minimises the associated risks and maximises the chances of success.

To address these challenges, an applied research project is being carried out at the Museu de Ciències Naturals de Barcelona (MCNB), in collaboration with the Universitat Politècnica de Catalunya (UPC). The aim of this project is to organise problems, questions and methodologies around this topic. Therefore, the main objective of this research is to design, generate and describe a comprehensive and specific strategic planning methodology for DT initiatives and their deployment, aimed at supporting the specific needs of NHMs, through an engineering qualitative study using the pragmatic approach of Design Science Research (DSR).

2 Current Challenges for Museums in Digital Transformation

2.1 The Covid19 Crisis as a Turning Point

The Covid19 pandemic disrupted the activities of museums worldwide, threatening their financial survival and the livelihoods of museum professionals [14]. During the closure, some museums were able to increase their digital activities, many of which built on pre-crisis investments, such as the digitisation of collections and the creation of digital/virtual museums [15]. The museum sector reacted very quickly during the pandemic to develop its online presence in order to maintain a link with the public.

During the lockdown and post-pandemic period, several studies were published on the impact of Covid19 on museums. Various sources, such as the International Council of Museums (ICOM) and the Network of European Museums Organisations (NEMO), agree on the importance of the need to train staff in digital and to rethink or develop a digital strategy in this new context [16]. As a result, the Covid19 crisis has forever changed museums' perception of the digital world, highlighting existing problems and accelerating changes that were already underway [17]. An increasing number of institutions are aware of the essential importance of digitisation and are offering digital experiences to the public, using various IS/IT as cyber-human systems. But the question now is: how to move from reaction to strategy?[18].

2.2 Educational Challenges

Digital transformation can be understood as the third stage in the adoption of digital technologies: digital competence $\rightarrow$ digital literacy $\rightarrow$ digital transformation [19]. This last stage means that digital uses inherently enable new types of innovation and creativity in a given domain, rather than merely enhancing and supporting traditional methods. Digital literacy is an organisational capability and consists of the ability of employees to use digital technologies in practices related to their work [20].

The digital literacy of the workforce is one of the key challenges for the adoption of technology in museums [12]. Increasing the digital literacy and confidence of museum professionals is a crucial aspect of supporting the DT initiatives in museums, creating a new mindset and enabling change. Museum professionals are challenged to develop new skills as IS/IT becomes more technically complex and the needs of their publics/audiences become more sophisticated [4, 21].

2.3 Interconnected Challenges

In addition, the Museum Sector Alliance (Mu.Sa) has detailed the critical issues and interrelated challenges faced by the museum sector in its DT processes [12]: lack of investment in digitisation of collections, limited investment in IS/IT infrastructure, lack of digital literacy of museum staff, insufficient training programmes, gaps in museum organisational structures to support digital maturity, lack of strategy or planning within digital activities, and government policies without clear guidelines to address digital challenges. Consequently, museums need to develop digital strategies to anchor their digitisation activities and digital assets on a sustainable and long-term basis in order to better achieve their mission and strategic goals [22].

3 Literature Review and Novelty

The museum and heritage sector has recently discussed the issue of DT as one of the main areas for its policy and research [23]. The types of studies are diverse. There are topics that have attracted the attention of academics, scholars and experts, such as the dissemination or didactics of cultural heritage. And there are other topics, such as digital networks between museums or strategic planning of DT, that have not generated as many references [24]. Consequently, there is not much literature on DT within cultural heritage institutions, and even less on their strategic planning of DT. This rather lack of prior research can be alleviated by research from other classic disciplines such as business management and information systems.

4 Applied Research at the Museu de Ciències Naturals de Barcelona (MCNB)

The MCNB and the UPC started an applied research project in July 2021, co-funded by the Generalitat de Catalunya and included in the Industrial Doctorate Plan. The starting point is the need for methods and guidelines to plan the strategy and successful implementation of DT initiatives in NHMs. It aims to contribute to this field of research with a comprehensive approach to risk mitigation and management, problem anticipation and overcoming of challenges faced by NHMs in their DT initiatives.

To this end, we chose to conduct a qualitative engineering study using a constructivist approach to design science research (DSR). A constructivist research approach (such as DSR) is a research process that aims to produce innovative constructs (artefacts) that are designed to solve real-world problems and, in doing so, make a theoretical contribution to the discipline in which it is applied [25]. DSR was chosen as the research approach because there is a practical problem that also has research potential due to the knowledge gap found in the literature. Therefore, by developing an artefact to solve the problem (a method), a theoretical contribution is made at the same time.

The model chosen to contextualise DSR in this research is the one presented by Hevner (2007). In this model, DSR is divided into three parts: environment, design science research and knowledge base. The environment has the practical domains: people, technical and organisational systems, with the problems and opportunities. In our research, the environment is represented by the MCNB, where the practice takes place and the designed solution is tested. In addition, the knowledge base is made up of the researcher's studies and experience, as well as the support provided by the University (UPC). The DSR process is located in the middle between theory and practice, where the artefact (the method) is designed and evaluated [26], see Fig. 1

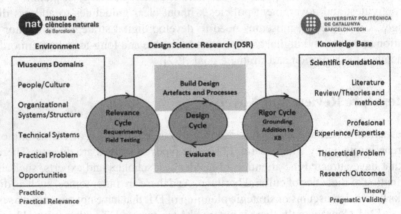

Fig. 1. DSR model. Source: adapted from Hevner (2007)

4.1 Research Design

As the main goal of this study is to design a method for strategic planning of DT and deployment in NHMs, the main expected outcome is a complete method and theoretical contribution made during its development, as well as its instantiation in a first strategic DT plan for the collection area of the MCNB [27]. In research design, the main goal was divided into five objectives (steps) related to the methodology to construct the artefact proposed by Manson [28] (see Fig. 2): problem awareness (O1), suggestion (O2), development (O3), evaluation (O4) and conclusion (O5).

In order to be aware of the problem (O1), a benchmarking study is carrying out on 16 reference NHMs worldwide to get more details on the context of NHMs (O1.1). Some of these are: Smithsonian National Museum of Natural History, Natural History Museum of London, Museum of Natural History (Berlin), Naturalis, etc.

In order to propose a solution (O2), it has been made a literature review to know the state of the problem and solutions about DT in NHMs (O2.1). In addition, it has been participated in digital projects within the MCNB (O2.2) to get more knowledge about the context of NHMs. In addition, a qualitative study on digital innovation in museums will be carried out by reviewing 1416 papers from the Museums and the Web proceedings, which is the main international conference on digital innovation in cultural heritage, to propose taxonomy of digital innovations in museums. As a result, a first version of the methodology can be proposed to start the development phase.

To develop the method (O3), it is necessary to identify and define the method requeriment (O3.1), the existing theories, models, methods and analysis tools to be included (O3.2), and to design the method phases and main components (O3.3). This will allow us to develop a second version of the method to for the evaluation phase.

To evaluate the method (O4), it will test and validate the design within the MCNB by doing its instantiation. It is also necessary to analyse if the method design is extensible to museums of other disciplines (O4.2). An evaluation by expert groups will allow us to make the final review to initiate the conclusion state.

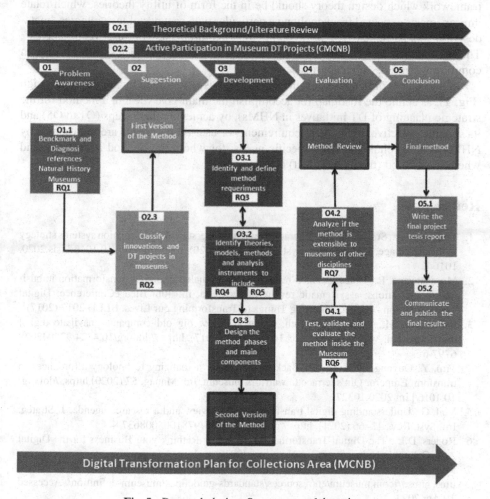

Fig. 2. Research design. Source: own elaboration

To conclude (O5), the final method will be presented, the final report (O5.1) and its publications (O5.2). Nevertheless, (O5.1) and (O5.2) are at the end, as long as results have come to light, they will be reported and published through the best channel. In addition, it is important to mention that O2.1, O2.2 and the DT plan for the MCNB are transversal for the whole design research. To date, the research project proposal has been successfully submitted to and approved by the UPC.

4.2   The Theorising or Theory Building Process

According to Veneable (2006), DSR must not leave theory and theorising to the natural and social (empirical) sciences. Instead, design science researchers should engage in theorising, before, during, and as a result of DSR work. As a result, he proposes an activity framework which design theory should be in the form of utility theories, which relate improvements expected from applying a particular type or types of technologies "meta-designs" to a particular type of problem "meta-requirements" or "user requirements". Theory and theorising/theory building are then seen as a central research activity, in common with all research approaches. [29].

In the context of this research, the meta-design is represented by the research design (Fig. 2), as define the roadmap for accomplish the main goal (design a method for the strategic planning of DT initiatives in NHMs), by achieving the 5 steps (O1 to O5) and its specific objectives. The meta-requirements or user-requirements are represented by NHMs context, challenges and specific needs; for whom the method is designed and where the method (the final artifact) is tested.

References

1. Teubner, R.A., Stockhinger, J.: Literature review: Understanding information systems strategy in the digital age. J. Strateg. Inf. Syst. **29**, 101642 (2020). https://doi.org/10.1016/j.jsis.2020.101642
2. Morakanyane, R., Grace, A.A., O'reilly, P.: Conceptualizing digital transformation in business organizations: a systematic review of literature. In: 30th Bled eConference: Digital Transformation - From Connecting Things to Transforming our Lives, BLED 2017 (2017)
3. Sebastian, I.M., Ross, J.W., Beath, C., et al.: How big old companies navigate digital transformation. MIS Quartely Exec. **16**, 197–213 (2017). https://doi.org/10.4324/9780429286797-6
4. Tim, Y., Ouyang, T., Zeng, D.: Back to the future: actualizing technology affordances to transform Emperor Qin's terracotta warriors museum. Inf. Manag. **57** (2020).https://doi.org/10.1016/j.im.2020.103271
5. Vial, G.: Understanding digital transformation: a review and a research agenda. J. Strateg. Inf. Syst. Rev., 13–66 (2021). https://doi.org/10.4324/9781003008637-4
6. Rogers, D.L.: The Digital Transformation Playbook: Rethink your Business for the Digital Age. Columbia University Press, New york (2016)
7. Museum Definition - International Council of Museums -International Council of Museums. https://icom.museum/en/resources/standards-guidelines/museum-definition/. Accessed 19 Apr 2023
8. Museos en la Era Digital – EVE Museos e Innovación. https://evemuseografia.com/2021/01/06/museos-en-la-era-digital/. Accessed 19 Apr 2023

9. Marty, P.F.: Museum informatics. In: Taylor & Francis (ed.) Encyclopedia of Library and Information Sciences, Third Edition, CRC Press, Boca Raton, pp 3717–3725 (2010)
10. Tong, Y., Ma, Y.: Digital museum construction standards study. In: International Archives of the Photogrammetry, Remote Sensing and Spatial Information Sciences - ISPRS Archives (2021)
11. Hossaini, A., Blankenberg, N.: Manual of Digital Museum Planning. Rowman & Littlefield, London (2017)
12. Mu.SA. The Future of Museum Professionals in the Digital Era, The Success Story of Mu.SA, First Edition. Hellenic Open University Press (2020)
13. Price, K., Dafydd, J.: Structuring for digital success: a global survey of how museums and other cultural organisations resource, fund, and structure their digital teams and activity. Museums Web 2018 (2020)
14. ICOM Museums, Museum Professionals and COVID-19 (2020)
15. UNESCO. Museums around the world: in the face of COVID-19. Paris, France (2020)
16. Rodà Llanza, C.: Capacitación digital de los profesionales de museos en plena transformación digital. In: Congreso CIMED. I Congreso internacional de Museos y Estrategias Digitales. Editorial Universitat Politècnica de València (2021)
17. ICOM. Museums, museum professionals and Covid-19: follow-up survey, vol. 34 (2020)
18. Culture 24. The Digital Transformation Agenda and GLAMs. A Quick Scan Report for Europeana (2020)
19. Baker, M.: Digital Transformation, Digital Ed. Buckingham Business Monographs, Buckingham (2014)
20. Cetindamar, D., Abedin, B., Shirahada, K.: The role of employees in digital transformation: a preliminary study on how employees' digital literacy impacts use of digital technologies. IEEE Trans. Eng. Manag. (2021). https://doi.org/10.1109/TEM.2021.3087724
21. Marty, P.F.: Museum websites and museum visitors : before and after the museum visit 22, 337–360 (2007). https://doi.org/10.1080/09647770701757708
22. NEMO. Final report Digitisation and IPR in European Museums (2020)
23. Liao, H.-T., Zhao, M., Sun, S.-P.: A literature review of museum and heritage on digitization, digitalization, and digital transformation. Adv. Soc. Sci. Educ. Humanit. Res. 435, 473–476 (2020). https://doi.org/10.2991/assehr.k.200428.101
24. Hurtado Jarandilla, A.: La dimensión digital de los museos españoles. Una cuestión ubicua. Universidad Carlos III de Madrid (2020)
25. Lukka, K.: The constructive research approach. In: Ojala, L., Hilmola, O.-P. (eds) In: Case study research in logistics. Turku School of Economics and Business Administration, pp 83–101 (2003)
26. Hevner, A.: A three cycle view of design science research. Scand. J. Inf. Syst. 19, 87–92 (2007). https://aisel.aisnet.org/sjis/vol19/iss2/4/
27. March, S.T., Smith, G.F.: Design and natural science research on information technology. Decis. Support. Syst. 15 (1995). https://doi.org/10.1016/0167-9236(94)00041-2
28. Manson, N.: Is operations research really research? Orion 22, 155–180 (2006). https://doi.org/10.5784/22-2-40
29. Venable, J.R.: The role of theory and theorising in design science research. In: Proceedings of the 1st International Conference on Design Science in Information Systems and Technology (DESRIST 2006) (2006)

The KYKLOS Tool for Modeling Changing Capabilities

Georgios Koutsopoulos(✉) ⬤, Martin Henkel ⬤, and Janis Stirna ⬤

Department of Computer and Systems Sciences, Stockholm University, Stockholm, Sweden
{georgios,martinh,js}@dsv.su.se

Abstract. Enterprise Modeling is a discipline that facilitates understanding and analyzing complex organizational phenomena and domains. A variety of methods and tools exist, often optimized for specific domains. KYKLOS is a domain-specific method that has been developed to model the phenomenon of changing business capabilities. It is not uncommon for such methods to be complemented by tools which facilitate the user and often enhance the method with additional technical functionalities. In this paper, the homonymous tool is presented, which has been developed using the ADOxx meta-modeling platform and complements the previously developed method.

Keywords: Capability · Change · Method · Tool · ADOxx · Adaptation · Transformation · Enterprise Modeling · Meta-modeling · Business Transformation

1 Introduction

The modern business environments pose a challenge for the organizations that operate within them, because of the existing high level of dynamism [1] that results in a continuous need to adapt what they are capable of, both on a strategic and operational level. Naturally, this makes the concept of capability management [2] and, more specifically, the phenomenon of changing business capabilities [3], highly relevant for the design and analysis involved in organizational research. As a response to this problem, a modeling method, namely KYKLOS [4], has been developed with the aim to tackle the phenomenon of changing capabilities.

A common practice within method design projects is to implement the methods in tools complementing the method, especially when it concerns conceptual modeling methods [5]. The aim of the implementation in tools is to enhance the method with the addition of automated functionalities integrated during the implementation [6], but also to facilitate the user's interaction with the tool while applying the method and improve the user's overall experience in the modeling environment. The result is the conversion of an implemented method to a toolkit, in other words, apart from the conceptual foundation and procedure, a platform for applying the method is provided.

The aim of this paper is to present the KYKLOS tool, which has been implemented in the ADOxx platform [7], emphasizing on the opportunities that emerged for enriching

C. Cabanillas and F. Perez (Eds.): CAiSE 2023, LNBIP 477, pp. 146–155, 2023.
https://doi.org/10.1007/978-3-031-34674-3_18

the specific method and improving the modeling experience of the user of the KYKLOS method. In parallel, the paper may provide design ideas for tool developers.

The rest of the paper is structured as follows. Section 2 provides a brief description of the related background, Sect. 3 presents the essential aspects of the tool, and Sect. 4 provides concluding remarks respectively.

2   Background

2.1   Development in a Meta-Modeling Platform

Developing a modeling method requires the development of a modeling technique and mechanisms and algorithms. The technique consists of a modeling language and a modeling procedure. The language consists of the syntax, semantics and notation [8]. A meta-modeling platform facilitates the implementation of all these components in a tool. A variety of platforms exist but the one selected for the development of the KYKLOS tool is ADOxx [7], provided by the Open Models Laboratory (OMiLAB).

The selection of ADOxx has been supported by the fact that its core platform enables different automation levels. Its benefits consist of its pre-existing functions and meta-model structure that help the developer save essential time and effort.

2.2   The KYKLOS Method

KYKLOS is a domain-specific capability modeling method [4], developed to tackle the phenomenon of changing business capabilities. Its extensive presentation is beyond the scope of this paper. Yet, the basic syntax, semantics and notation are presented in Sect. 3, thus, here, we delimit the description to the summarized requirements that the method addresses, and its modeling procedure. The complete set of requirements of KYKLOS consists of 28 goals [9], summarized in the following areas (i) Intentions, (ii) Context, (iii) Decision-making, (iv) Capability components, (v) Transitions, (vi) Capability and component ownership, and Capability associations.

KYKLOS's modeling procedure consists of four phases, (i) the Foundation, where the analyzed capability and its outcomes are modeled, (ii) the Observation, where the capability's context is modeled, along with the organization's intentions that are fulfilled by the capability, as a means to capture the need to change, (iii) the Decision alternatives, where the various alternative configurations of the capability are formulated and analyzed, along with the allocation and ownership status of the components that comprise each configuration, and (iv), the Delivery, where the change and its properties [10] are captured as a transition between configurations.

3   The KYKLOS Tool

3.1   Syntax

The syntax is presented as a Tool meta-model. It is an enriched version of the KYKLOS Language meta-model, which is published in [4, 6] and not presented here due to the page limits. The enrichment consists only of function-related concepts. The Tool meta-model (Fig. 1) includes color-coding to distinguish the language concepts (orange), the edited language concepts (red) and the function-related concepts (blue).

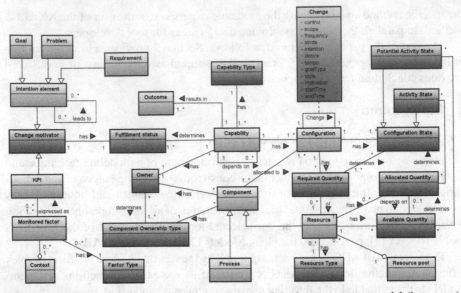

Fig. 1. The Tool meta-model. It retains the concepts of the Language meta-model (in orange), concepts that have been modified (in red), and new function-related concepts (in blue).

3.2 Semantics

The description of the included concepts (semantics) of the tool, is presented in Table 1. The upper part describes the language concepts and the lower part describes the function-related concepts that have been added during the implementation.

Table 1. The complete set of language concepts and their definitions, adapted from [4].

Concept	Description
Language concepts	
Capability	A capability is a potential to create value by fulfilling an intention within a context, using resources and behaviors
Configuration	The set of resources used by the capability along with the behavior elements that deliver it. A capability may have several different configurations but only one may be active at any given moment in time
Resource	Any type of asset that is used by an organization to enable the capability's realization. It can be allocated to one or more capability configurations, based on its capacity
Resource pool	The complete set of an organization's available resources

(continued)

Table 1. (*continued*)

Concept	Description
Context	All the factors that form the setting in which a capability exists, are relevant to its performance and within which the capability is perceived
Outcome	The result of the capability's realization
KPI	A preset measurable value that expresses an important aspect of the context
Monitored Factor	A context factor that has been identified and associated to a capability's performance and is being observed in relation to the capability. It is usually expressed as a KPI
Intention element	An abstract element that includes all the concepts that refer to the intentions governing the capability, for example, goals, problems or requirements
Goal	A desirable state that an organization aims to achieve. It is a type of Intention element
Problem	An undesirable condition that an organization aims to avoid or tackle
Requirement	A necessary state that an organization has to fulfill. It is a type of Intention element
Process	A behavior element that consists of activities aiming to fulfill a certain goal
Change	Change represents the transition from one configuration to another and its properties
Function-related concepts	
Configuration state	This concept captures the generalization of Activity and Potential activity states
Activity state	This concept has been added to show dynamically when a configuration is active
Potential activity state	This concept enables the user to know when a configuration is ready to be active via resource reallocation
Available quantity	This concept captures the tool's functionality to identify all the available resources in the model
Allocated quantity	Allocated quantity captures the resources that have been properly allocated to a configuration that requires them
Required quantity	This addition captures the tool's function to identify the resources that the configuration requires for its activation

(*continued*)

Table 1. (*continued*)

Concept	Description
Change motivator	This is a generalization of KPIs and Intention elements and has been added to capture the common treatment of these elements as decision criteria
Fulfillment status	This functionality depicts the dynamic visualization of the association between change motivators and the associated capability
Factor type	It identifies the captured type of a factor that is associated to a capability via its KPI(s)
Capability type	This functionality has been added as part of the component ownership function that classifies capabilities between main and supporting ones
Owner	Captures the ownership of components and capabilities
Resource type	Captures the type of a resource that is associated to a capability via its KPI(s)
Component ownership type	The concept allows to capture automatically whether a component is owned internally or externally

3.3 Graphical Notation

A previously mentioned component of a modeling language and method is the notation. The KYKLOS tool uses a graphical notation developed specifically for the method (Table 2).

Table 2. The graphical notation of KYKLOS, from [4].

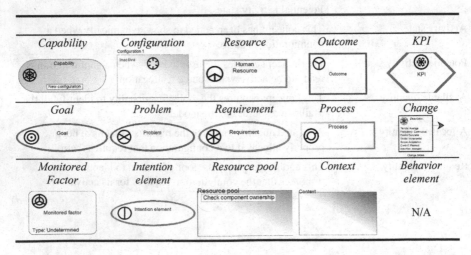

3.4 Functionalities

This section describes additions that facilitate the user's experience while modeling in the tool and enrich the modeling method.

User Experience Functionalities

New Configuration. On every capability object, there is a button that creates a new configuration object. The new object is also automatically connected. Its spatial alignment is taken into consideration for higher visual quality. The function creates a configuration, a relationship connecting the source capability with the created configuration, and positions the object so that no overlapping occurs. New objects are assigned named based on the number of existing Configurations to avoid name duplication (Fig. 2).

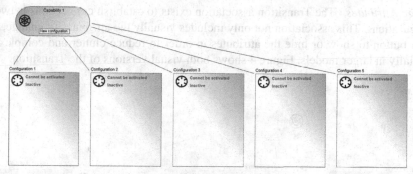

Fig. 2. The create configuration functionality in KYKLOS, used for multiple objects.

Containment & Prevention of Loose Components: An element that is graphically inside another one triggers an invisible "inside" relationship, which means that connecting lines are not required, leading to a reduced number of crossing lines. The positions of a container and an "inside" object are checked using the container's borders. KYKLOS prevents the existence of "outside" components. A contained object moves along with a moving container to remain inside and in any attempt to move it "outside", the object returns to its last position. Also, new components cannot be created while not inside a container. The tool also informs the user about this state, as shown in Fig. 3.

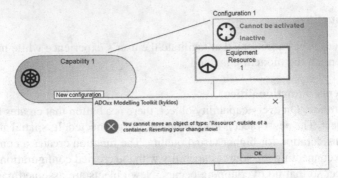

Fig. 3. Containtment and Prevention of loose components in KYKLOS.

Change Attributes. The Transition association exists to establish connections between configurations. This association not only includes visually the attributes of change, but also a button to show or hide the attributes in order to reduce clutter and complexity, especially in larger models. Figure 4 shows both visual versions of the Transition.

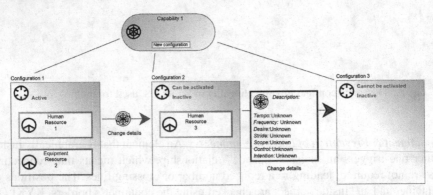

Fig. 4. The two visualizations of the attributes of change in KYKLOS.

Relationship Grouping. A plethora of association types would normally exist in the tool, yet, in order to avoid this situation, all associations but Status and Change share visualizations. Yet, the tool includes rules for preventing using wrong associations. This mitigates the risk of mistakes. This functionality is shown in Fig. 5.

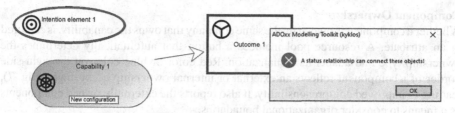

Fig. 5. Relationship grouping in KYKLOS.

Method Enrichment Functionalities

Configuration Activation. The allocation of the required components in a configuration determines if it is active or not. In the tool, allocation is translated as containment in a container. The required components are documented in a "Notebook" area of a Configuration object. This allows a user to specify the necessary components for activating the capability (Fig. 6). The tool compares required and allocated components in a configuration and activates or deactivates it. The tool also checks the entire modeling area and identifies if the required resources exist in the model, even if they are not allocated to the given configuration of the capability. This provides an additional functionality, since the tool suggests if and when a configuration can be activated (see Fig. 7).

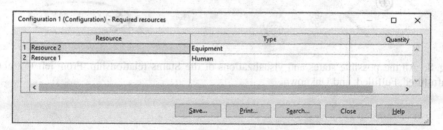

Fig. 6. Specification of required resources in a configuration's Notebook.

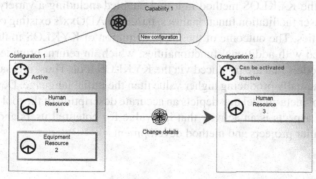

Fig. 7. Configuration activity and potential activity states, using the contained resources. Automatic color-coding of resources to show internal (blue) or external (red) ownership.

Component Ownership

Whether a component is owned by the same company that owns the capability, is captured in an attribute. A resource pool includes a button that automatically determines the ownership type and adapts its visualization. Red color or blue color on the right-side border of a component reflects an external or internal ownership accordingly (Fig. 7), leading to improved comprehensibility. It also reports the externally owned components as a means to consider organizational boundaries.

Decision Motivation

A special association called Status connects a capability with KPIs and all types of Intention elements. The capability may fulfill or not the content of the connected object and this determines the visualization of Status to facilitate the identification of a need to change. This dynamic visualization is using the Fulfillment attribute, and its possible values, "Fulfilled", "Unfulfilled", and "Unknown" (Fig. 8).

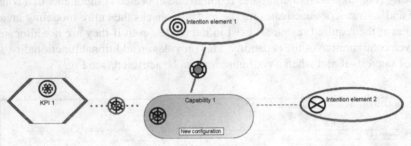

Fig. 8. All the possible states and visualizations of the Status relationship. From left to right, Unfulfilled, Fulfilled, and Unknown.

4   Conclusion

Implementing the KYKLOS method in a tool enabled including a variety of method-enriching and user facilitation functionalities, based on ADOxx's existing core structure and functionalities. The outcome of the implementation of KYKLOS in the tool was a method enriched with additional functionalities, which, in return, provided a dynamic aspect to the models that are produced via the KYKLOS tool. Thus, it is safe to assume that the tool is actually producing higher value than the initial language. Developing and presenting a tool meta-model that depicts an accurate description of the tool and captures all its dynamic aspects is an activity that has value for potential users and researchers involved in similar projects and method development.

References

1. Burke, W.W.: Organization Change: Theory and Practice. Sage Publications, Sage Publications (2017)

2. Sandkuhl, K., Stirna, J. eds.: Capability Management in Digital Enterprises. Springer International Publishing, Cham (2018). https://doi.org/10.1007/978-3-319-90424-5

3. Koutsopoulos, G.: Managing capability change in organizations: foundations for a modeling approach. http://urn.kb.se/resolve?urn=urn:nbn:se:su:diva-185231. (2020)

4. Koutsopoulos, G., Henkel, M., Stirna, J.: Modeling the phenomenon of capability change: the KYKLOS method. In: Karagiannis, D., Lee, M., Hinkelmann, K., Utz, W. (eds.) Domain-Specific Conceptual Modeling, pp. 265–288. Springer, Cham (2022)

5. Karagiannis, D., Lee, M., Hinkelmann, K., Utz, W. (eds.): Domain-Specific Conceptual Modeling: Concepts Methods and ADOxx Tools. Springer, Cham (2022)

6. Koutsopoulos, G., Henkel, M.: An experience report on the implementation of the KYKLOS modeling method. In: Serral, E., Stirna, J., Ralyté, J., Grabis, J. (eds.) PoEM 2021. LNBIP, vol. 432, pp. 103–118. Springer, Cham (2021). https://doi.org/10.1007/978-3-030-91279-6_8

7. OMiLAB: The ADOxx Metamodelling Platform. https://www.adoxx.org/live/home

8. Karagiannis, D., Kühn, H.: Metamodelling Platforms. In: Bauknecht, K., Tjoa, A.M., Quirch-mayr, G. (eds.) EC-Web 2002. LNCS, vol. 2455, pp. 182–182. Springer, Heidelberg (2002). https://doi.org/10.1007/3-540-45705-4_19

9. Koutsopoulos, G., Henkel, M., Stirna, J.: Requirements for observing, deciding, and delivering capability change. In: Gordijn, J., Guédria, W., Proper, H.A. (eds.) PoEM 2019. LNBIP, vol. 369, pp. 20–35. Springer, Cham (2019). https://doi.org/10.1007/978-3-030-35151-9_2

10. Koutsopoulos, G., Henkel, M., Stirna, J.: Modeling the dichotomies of organizational change: a state-based capability typology. In: Feltus, C., Johannesson, P., and Proper, H.A. (eds.) PoEM 2019 Forum, pp. 26–39. CEUR-WS.org, Luxembourg (2020)

Author Index

C. Cabanillas and F. Perez (Eds.): CAiSE 2023, LNBIP 477, pp. 157–158, 2023.
https://doi.org/10.1007/978-3-031-34674-3

Printed in the United States
by Baker & Taylor Publisher Services